Your 10-Day Spiritual Action Plan for

Faith
That Can Move
Mountains

KENNETH
COPELAND
PUBLICATIONS

by Kenneth and Gloria
Copeland

Includes material from the *Believer's Voice of Victory* magazine, *God's Will Is Prosperity, The Laws of Prosperity, Blessed to Be a Blessing* (formerly published as *Managing God's Mutual Funds—Yours and His*), *One Word From God Can Change Your Finances, Prosperity: The Choice Is Yours, Prosperity Promises,* Kenneth Copeland's Partner Letters, as well as newly created content and interactive action plans inspired by these resources.

Your 10-Day Spiritual Action Plan for Faith That Can Move Mountains

ISBN: 978-1-60463-246-0   30-3040

19 18 17 16 15 14   7 6 5 4 3 2

© 2013 Eagle Mountain International Church Inc. aka Kenneth Copeland Ministries

For more information about Kenneth Copeland Ministries, visit kcm.org or call 1-800-600-7395 (U.S. only) or +1-817-852-6000.

CD Credits:

Executive Producers | Kenneth and Gloria Copeland
Produced by | Robert Wirtz
Engineered, Mixed & Mastered by | Robert Wirtz for Eagle Mountain Productions
Assistant Engineer | Michael Phelps
Production Assistant | Christen McCarley
Recorded at | Eagle Mountain Recording Studio, Newark, Texas; Front Room Studio, Keller, Texas; and Michael Howell Productions, Fort Worth, Texas

Faith Is

Beckah Shae & Jonathan Shocklee
Shae Shoc Publishing (ASCAP)

Worship Leader—Aubrey Oaks | Drums—Chad Whitely | Bass—Darrell Wren | Guitars—Michael Phelps | Acoustic Guitars—Michael Howell | Keyboards—Clay Collins | Additional Keyboards & Programming—Robert Wirtz | Background Vocals—Melissa Spangler

Let God Arise

Chris Tomlin, Jesse Reeves, Ed Cash
© 2006 worshiptogether.com Songs (ASCAP) sixsteps Music (ASCAP) Vamos Publishing (ASCAP) (adm. at EMICMGPublishing.com) / FORMERLY ALLETROP (BMI) All rights reserved. Used by permission.

Worship Leader—Jeff Spangler | Drums—Chad Whitely | Bass—Darrell Wren | Guitars—Michael Phelps | Acoustic Guitars—Michael Howell | Keyboards—Clay Collins | Additional Keyboards & Programming—Robert Wirtz | Background Vocals—Christen McCarley, Jeff Spangler, Melissa Spangler, Robert Wirtz

Nothing Is Impossible

Joth Hunt
© 2011 Planet Shakers Ministries International Inc. (ASCAP) (adm. at EMICMGPublishing.com) All rights reserved. Used by permission.

Worship Leader—Jeff Spangler & Melissa Spangler | Drums—Chad Whitely | Bass—Darrell Wren | Guitars—Michael Phelps | Acoustic Guitars | Michael Howell | Keyboards—Clay Collins | Additional Keyboards & Programming—Robert Wirtz | Background Vocals—Christen McCarley, Jeff Spangler, Melissa Spangler, Robert Wirtz

In Christ Alone

Keith Getty, Stuart Townend
© 2002 Thankyou Music (PRS) (adm. worldwide at EMICMGPublishing.com excluding Europe which is adm. by Kingswaysongs) All rights reserved. Used by permission.

Worship Leader—Max Kutz | Drums—Chad Whitely | Bass—Darrell Wren | Guitars & Banjo—Michael Phelps | Acoustic Guitars—Michael Howell | Keyboards—Clay Collins Additional Keyboards & Programming—Robert Wirtz | Background Vocals—Jenny Kutz, Christen McCarley

Weakness for Strength

Michael Howell & Sherrie Howell
©2011 Dive Deep Music | Master Track used by permission of Dive Deep Music

Worship Leader— Michael Howell | Keyboards & Programming—Michael Howell, Sherrie Howell | Electric Guitars—Michael Phelps, Michael Howell | Acoustic Guitars—Michael Howell | Bass—Michael Howell | Drums—Nicholas Leitzinger | Background Vocals—Sherrie Howell, Michael Howell

One Thing Remains (Your Love Never Fails)

Brian Johnson, Jeremy Riddle, Christa Black
© 2010 Bethel Music Publishing (ASCAP)/Mercy Vineyard Publishing (ASCAP) (adm. by Music Services)/ Christajoy Music (BMI) (Admin by Bethel Music Publishing). All rights reserved. Used by permission.

Worship Leader—Michael Phelps | Drums—Chad Whitely | Bass—Darrell Wren | Guitars & Banjo—Michael Phelps | Acoustic Guitars—Michael Howell | Keyboards—Clay Collins Additional Keyboards & Programming—Robert Wirtz | Background Vocals—Christen McCarley

The Anthem/Hallelujah

Henry Seeley, Joth Hunt, Liz Webber

Worship Leader—Jeff Spangler | Drums—Chad Whitely | Bass—Darrell Wren | Guitars—Michael Phelps | Acoustic Guitars—Michael Howell | Keyboards—Clay Collins | Additional Keyboards & Programming—Robert Wirtz | Background Vocals—Christen McCarley, Melissa Spangler, Robert Wirtz

No Chains on Me

Chris Tomlin, Jesse Reeves, Ed Cash

Worship Leader—Christen McCarley | Drums—Chad Whitely | Bass—Darrell Wren | Guitars—Michael Phelps | Acoustic Guitars—Michael Howell | Keyboards—Clay Collins | Additional Keyboards & Programming—Robert Wirtz | Background Vocals—Christen McCarley, Melissa Spangler, Robert Wirtz

Never Once

Matt Redman

Worship Leader—Jeff Spangler | Drums—Chad Whitely | Bass—Darrell Wren | Guitars—Michael Phelps | Acoustic Guitars—Michael Howell | Keyboards—Clay Collins | Additional Keyboards & Programming—Robert Wirtz | Background Vocals—Christen McCarley

We Have Overcome

Israel Houghton & Meleasa Houghton

Worship Leader—Melissa Spangler | Drums—Chad Whitely | Bass—Darrell Wren | Guitars—Michael Phelps | Acoustic Guitars—Michael Howell | Keyboards—Clay Collins | Additional Keyboards & Programming—Robert Wirtz | Background Vocals—Christen McCarley, Melissa Spangler, Robert Wirtz

Table of
Contents

Quick-Start Guide

LifeLine

Practical Tools for Everyday Needs

To start developing your faith *now,* follow this **Quick-Start Guide...**

Your faith—and yes, every born-again believer possesses faith—has the potential to produce the same results Jesus produced in His earthly ministry (John 14:12). Faith is a lifestyle, but if you need to jump-start yours for a breakthrough—*fast*—begin with the following steps, today:

1. Begin fellowshiping with the Father regularly.

Your relationship with The LORD is the most important aspect of your faith walk. Get to know Him through His WORD and prayer by spending quality time alone with Him. Let Him reveal Himself to you!

2. Meditate on and confess The WORD of God.

Meditation and confession go hand in hand (Joshua 1:8). What you meditate on regulates what you believe. What you confess with your mouth sets the course for your actions. Meditation and confession will allow you to believe God's WORD enough to act on it in faith. (You can start with the scriptures in Appendix B of this book.)

3. Pray in the spirit

Jude 20 says, "But ye, beloved, building up yourselves on your most holy faith, praying in the Holy Ghost." Praying in the spirit is a spiritual exercise that builds up your most holy faith. As you spend time every day praying in your prayer language, you keep your spirit active rather than passive.

4. Make the quality decision to live by faith.

To develop your faith, you must make a quality decision—a decision from which there is no retreat—that you, with God's help, will never violate. It's a decision you must hold to no matter what you face or what others say or do.

5. Walk in love.

Faith works by love (Galatians 5:6). If you're not walking in love with others, or have unforgiveness in your heart, it will stop your faith cold. Choose to walk in love.

While you're taking these steps and stirring up your faith, work through this *10-Day Spiritual Action Plan*. Soon, you'll see that as you build your faith, with the help of this LifeLine Kit, your whole world will change for the better!

Your Quick-Start Prayer

Father, I begin my journey today, walking by faith and not by sight. You have given me the measure of faith (Romans 12:3), and now help me to develop it as I listen to Your WORD. Let that WORD penetrate my heart so deeply that it begins to flow out of my mouth in faith.

By faith, now, I speak boldly to this mountain I'm facing: "(Call the mountain by name.) _____, be removed! Be cast into the sea!"

*I know these words **will** come to pass because Your WORD in Mark 11:23-24 says so. I know it because I am choosing to walk in love, and I believe Your WORD is true. I know it because You, LORD, are faithful.*

In the Name of Jesus. Amen!

Your Faith Promises

- Hebrews 11:1
- Romans 12:3
- Romans 10:17
- Galatians 5:6
- Mark 11:22-23

You will find more prayers, confessions and scriptures listed in the back of this book.

How to Use
Your LifeLine Kit

How to Use
Your LifeLine Kit

We believe *Your 10-Day Spiritual Action Plan for Faith That Can Move Mountains* will give you the power tools to stand in the faith God has given you—for every break-through you need.

To accomplish this, we've created one of the most in-depth resources, with step-by-step guidance, that Kenneth Copeland Ministries has ever made available on this subject—all in one place. Here are some practical tips to get you started and help you make the most of this kit:

- Commit to making the next 10 days *your* days for renewing your mind. Set aside any distractions and be prepared to make adjustments in your life so you can get the most out of this kit.

- This plan should be a blessing, not a burden. If you miss a day or can't quite get through one day's materials, just start where you left off at your next op-portunity. If you have to, be flexible with the kit to ensure you make it to the end. If you only have half an hour a day, that's fine—commit that! It may take longer to complete the kit, but you can be confident those 30 days will still be some of the most life-changing days you've ever had.

- Use this LifeLine workbook as your starting point each day, to guide your reading, listening, watching and journaling. Before you know it, your life will be saturated with God's WORD like never before.

- We recommend that you:

  > ▶ **Read and journal** in the morning
  > ▶ **Meditate** on the scriptures daily
  > ▶ **Use** the CD and DVD products daily
  >   as instructed in each chapter
  > ▶ **Read and journal** again at night

- Remember, the goal is to do a little every day. Steady doses are the best medicine.

- This is an action book! Have a pen handy to underline and take notes.

- Fully engage with all the materials. Write in your workbook, speak the scrip-tures, pray the prayers, sing with the music and take time to enjoy the materials in every way.

- Carry your daily action card and refer to it throughout your day as a point of connection with God.

- Make your study time focused. Do your best to remove distractions and find a quiet place.

You're closer than ever to developing the kind of faith you've always wanted: *Faith That Can Move Mountains.*

Always remember that God loves you and He is *for* you. We're standing with you, and "Jesus Is Lord!"

Chapter One
What Faith Is

Wake Up Your Faith!
by Kenneth Copeland

I'm so glad you picked up this LifeLine Kit about faith because faith changed my life. It also changed Gloria's life and the lives of all our children and grandchildren *forever* because we have chosen to live our lives believing God's WORD, unconditionally. In other words, we live *by faith.*

That's important, because you'll see throughout this kit that receiving anything from God is done *with* and *by* faith.

And, if you want to live a victorious life, you'll want to live by faith, too.

What is faith? Hebrews 11:1 states, "Now faith is the substance of things hoped for, the evidence of things not seen."

Faith is the connector between God and man. Hebrews 11:6 says, "Without faith it is impossible to please him: for he that cometh to God must believe that he is, and that he is a rewarder of them that diligently seek him." It is impossible to please God without faith. Why? Because your Father is not pleased when He cannot manifest Himself in your life and meet your needs.

Since faith is the connection by which salvation, healing, financial prosperity and more are transferred from heaven to you, it's impossible to please Him without it. Jesus went through the horrible death of the cross and suffered in hell so all our needs could be met according to His riches in glory. Then, He made available, to you, His faith by which to receive.

Let's look closer at how faith comes to you.

First, let's look at Romans 10:6-13:

But the righteousness which is of faith speaketh on this wise, Say not in thine heart, Who shall ascend into heaven? (that is, to bring Christ down from above:) Or, Who shall descend into the deep? (that is, to bring up Christ again from the dead.) But what saith it? The WORD is nigh thee, even in thy mouth, and in thy heart: that is, The WORD of faith, which we preach; That if thou shalt confess with thy mouth The LORD Jesus, and shalt believe in thine heart that God hath raised him from the dead, thou shalt be saved. For with the heart man believeth unto righteousness; and with the mouth confession is made unto salvation. For the scripture saith, Whosoever believeth on him shall not be ashamed. For there is no difference between the Jew and the Greek: for the same LORD over all is rich unto all that call upon him. For *whosoever* shall call upon the name of The LORD shall be saved.

Faith is available for "whosoever." Whosoever, that is, who will obey the laws that govern it. Whosoever means you and me!

How does faith come to you and me? Romans 10:17 states, "So then faith cometh by hearing, and hearing by The WORD of God." God's WORD is the source of God's faith. (We'll look much closer at this truth in Chapter 4 of this LifeLine Kit, but it's an important point for you to remember that right now.)

Everything God has, His very best, is always available to the claim of faith. No one has to sit and wait for some kind of special move of God, or for some special anointing to fall, in order to receive healing or a breakthrough. God is ready, now. He's always on. He's always saving. He's always healing. His abundance is always at hand. It is nigh thee, even in thy mouth. There's a miracle in your mouth just waiting to be released.

Words alone are not enough. They must be filled with faith.

Feeble Faith

Here's the problem: Low-level, feeble faith (meaning either faith that hasn't been fed by God's WORD, or faith that has been contaminated because it has been mixed with fear) will allow the enemy into your life. Remember, Ephesians 6:16, talking about the full armor of God, says, "Above all, taking the shield of faith, wherewith ye shall be able to quench *all* the fiery darts [or weapons] of the wicked." The rest of the armor depends on faith to work. The helmet of salvation, breastplate of righteousness, etc., work by faith.

Without the shield of faith, you're uncovered. You're especially vulnerable where your physical body is concerned. It becomes very difficult to hold on strongly to your faith confession when pain strikes. Even when you do say the right things, they can bring little result because they can be mental, empty words. Then, it's easy to begin to question God: *Why doesn't He help me with this? I wonder what's wrong, here?* That's when things get worse instead of better.

It's time—or really past time—to get under The WORD of faith and *stay there* night and day. Put everything else aside.

Let me say that again: *Put everything else aside.*

There's nothing more important.

NOTHING.

Shout the Truth

It's time to wake up your faith. It's time to wake up the strong man, the giant that's asleep inside your innermost being. I know you believe that, too, or you wouldn't have picked up this book.

So, let's do it!

Look pain and failure in the eye and *shout*. It's very, very important to *shout* with every fiber of your being. I mean it, now—you'll have to do it!

In fact, let's test this right now. Just say in a normal but firm tone, "Greater is He that is in me than he that is in the world."

Now check out your level of faith. Notice your inner condition.

Next, take a deep breath and *shout those words with everything you've got. I mean, everything!* 1-2-3-SHOUT!

"GREATER IS HE THAT IS IN ME THAN HE THAT IS IN THE WORLD!"

Check yourself out again. Wow! The giant's awake! Let him roar!

Let faith talk. Say:

"I'M A FREE MAN! I'M COMING OUT OF THE CAGE! JESUS HAS SET ME FREE! I'M SUPPOSED

TO PROSPER! I'M SUPPOSED TO BE HEALED! I'M SUPPOSED TO BE HAPPY AND FILLED WITH JOY! I REFUSE TO GO BACK INTO THAT CAGE OF DOUBT AND UNBELIEF!"

Now that your faith is awake, talk right now about how wonderful your heavenly Father is. Praise Him. Tell Him how grateful you are that you're free. Say, "Thank God, I'm not going to hell!" Don't talk about the devil anymore. Give him no place.

God's Part/Our Part

Romans 3:27 says faith works by spiritual law—the law of faith.

Galatians 5:6 says faith works by love. Jesus said in Matthew 22:37, "Thou shalt love The LORD thy God with all thy heart, and with all thy soul, and with all thy mind."

The law of faith hinges on the commandment of love just like all the rest of the law and the prophets. Nothing that's of God works without love. (Of course not! God is love. Nothing *of* God works *without* God.)

So, let's put Romans 10:17 and Galatians 5:6 together and we'll see both our part and God's part in developing our faith:

Faith cometh = that's God's part.
By hearing = that's our part.
Faith worketh = that's God's part.
By love = that's our part.

Make the quality decision that must be made so you'll never be in that weakened position, ever again: "I will keep the commandment of love. I will stay in The WORD and live by faith."

Get yourself in line with what faith truly is—what The WORD says it is—and watch your life forever change!

Morning Reflection

Define faith.

_____

_____

Why is faith so important?

_____

_____

According to Romans 10:17 and Galatians 5:6, what is your responsibility in building your faith? How are you going to begin implementing it?

_____

_____

_____

Today's Connection Points

- **Faith That Can Move Mountains CD: "Faith Is" (Track 1)**

  "Faith Is" being sure of what you hope for. It's the certainty of unseen things!

- **DVD: "The Force of Faith" (Chapter 1)**

  Faith works the same way every time: by hearing and feeding on The WORD of God. Kenneth explains how to activate the God-kind of faith that dwells in you!

- **Faith Scriptures CD (Track 1)**

  Hebrews 11:1-3, 6; Romans 10:6-12, 13-17; Ephesians 6:16; Romans 3:27; Galatians 5:6; Romans 4:3; 2 Corinthians 4:18

Faith in Action

Begin reading and meditating on The WORD of God.
Then begin speaking—and shouting out—the promises your heavenly Father has given you through His WORD.

Notes:

_____

_____

_____

_____

_____

_____

_____

_____

_____

_____

_____

_____

_____

_____

_____

_____

_____

_____

The Unbeatable Spirit of Faith

by Gloria Copeland

I'm so glad you've picked up this LifeLine Kit about faith. Because no matter how difficult the situation you may be facing today, there's something I want you to know: *God can turn it around!*

The doctors may have told you there's no hope. Your bank account may be empty, and creditors knocking on your door. There may be trouble in your family or on your job. Your problems may be stacked so high, you feel you can never overcome them. But don't let the devil fool you. He has never devised a problem that faith in God can't fix.

Nothing intimidates God. It's just as easy for Him to heal cancer as it is for Him to heal a headache. It's as easy for Him to buy you a new home as it is for Him to pay your rent.

Even in times like these when the whole world seems to be in trouble, God can bring you through in triumph. He can do for you what He did for the Israelites. Exodus 10:23 says when darkness covered the land of Egypt where the Israelites lived—a darkness so thick the Egyptians couldn't see each other or move for three days—"all the children of Israel had light in their dwellings."

Think about that! If you'll dare to believe God's WORD, like the Israelites, you too can have light in the middle of a dark world. You can have protection in the midst of a dangerous world. You can live healed in a sick world. You can live prosperously in an impoverished world. You can live free in the middle of a captive world.

But you can't do it by dragging around in an attitude of defeat. If you want to walk in constant victory, you must develop a spirit of faith and persevere in that spirit even when the devil is putting pressure on you.

People with the spirit of faith always receive the blessings of God. They may go through tests and trials but they come out supernaturally every time.

I like those odds, don't you? I like to beat the devil every time. And, glory to God, you and I can do that if we'll walk continually in the spirit of faith.

The Faith Connection

That, by the way, is why it's so important to develop your faith: because faith is what connects you to the blessings of God. It's the force that gives those blessings substance in your life (see Hebrews 11:1). And, besides all that, faith pleases God (Hebrews 11:6).

It's faith that reaches into the realm of the spirit, grasps the promises of God and brings forth a tangible, physical fulfillment of those promises. It brings spiritual blessings. It brings the car you need, or healing for your body. Faith brings action in this earth.

Romans 5:2 says we have access by faith into the grace of God. Therefore, if you want grace for the new birth, you must receive it by faith. If you want God's grace for healing, you must receive it by faith. If you want God's grace in your finances or any other area of your life, you must receive it by faith.

I like to think of it this way: When you believe The WORD of God, you open the window of your life to give God the opportunity to move there.

Oddly enough, that bothers some people. They can't understand why God needs *an opportunity*. After all, He is God. Can't He do anything He wants to?

Yes, He can. And He wants to respond to our faith.

You see, He's not like the devil. He doesn't force Himself on you. He waits for you to give Him an opening by believing His WORD.

Keep Your Eyes on The WORD

That's what Abraham did. When God told him he and Sarah were going to have a baby, Abraham just took God at His WORD. In light of the circumstances, that was quite a step of faith. After all, Abraham was 100 years old and Sarah was 90 and barren.

Most people would have been overwhelmed by those problems. But not Abraham. He "believed God, and it was counted unto him for righteousness" (Romans 4:3). Even though in the natural realm, it was impossible for what God said to come to pass, Abraham believed God anyway.

That's what the spirit of faith does. It stands in the midst of the most impossible circumstances and believes God anyway!

Right now you may be thinking, *I really want to do that. I want to live by faith. The problem is, every time I look at the mess I'm in, I get discouraged.*

Then, stop looking at the mess! Instead, focus your attention on the promises of God. Keep His WORD in front of your eyes and in your ears until you can *see* it coming to pass with the eyes of your spirit.

That's what the spirit of faith does. It looks "not at the things which are seen, but at the things which are not seen: for the things which are seen are temporal; but the things which are not seen are eternal" (2 Corinthians 4:18).

Of course, I'm not saying you should ignore your problems or close your eyes to them as if they aren't real. They are real. But, according to The WORD of God, they are *temporal,* which means "subject to change." And, you can be assured that if you keep looking at The WORD, they *will* change!

Once again, we can look at Abraham's life and see proof of that. Romans 4:18-21 says that he:

Against hope believed in hope, that he might become the father of many nations, according to that which was spoken, So shall thy seed be. And being not weak in faith, he considered not his own body now dead, when he was about an hundred years old, neither yet the deadness of Sarah's womb: He staggered not at the promise of God through unbelief; but was strong in faith, giving glory to God; and being fully persuaded that, what he had promised, he was able also to perform.

Abraham did not consider his body. He didn't focus his attention on the fact that he was 100 years old. He wasn't looking at his wrinkled, old self, saying, "Come on, old man. You can do it!" No, he knew he couldn't bring forth a child. He'd known that for some time.

He wasn't looking at his own ability. He was looking at God's. He kept his attention on the power and promise of God until he was fully persuaded that God could *and would* bring it to pass.

That's What I Call Victory!

If you want to develop the spirit of faith, that's what you'll do, too. You won't consider the natural impossibilities of your situation—God certainly doesn't. Ken and I have found that out by experience!

More than 45 years ago, when Ken was praying, down in a riverbed in Tulsa, Oklahoma, God began speaking to him about preaching to nations. God said back then that Ken would have a worldwide ministry.

It was clear God had not considered our bank account. We hardly had enough money to get across town—much less go to the nations! But God didn't expect *us* to fulfill that call. He intended to do it Himself with our faith. He intended to provide the power, the resources, the ability—everything! All He expected us to do was believe.

That's all He expects you to do, too. *Only believe.*

Isn't that wonderfully simple?

If you'll just believe, if you'll just spend your time considering God's WORD instead of focusing on your own limitations, you'll end up just like Abraham.

Exactly how did Abraham end up? Very well, I'd say.

He and Sarah not only had that baby God promised, they also lived long enough to raise him. Then, after Sarah died at 127 years old, Abraham (who was 137) remarried and had six more children. He became exactly what he and God said he was—the father of many nations.

Now, that's what I call victory!

That's what I call the *spirit of faith!*

Evening Reflection

For what situation are you standing in faith? (Healing? Financial breakthrough? A family situation?)

_____

_____

_____

_____

What does The WORD say about your situation? Find 3-5 scriptures on which to stand.

_____

_____

_____

Write your confession for that situation, based on those scriptures.

_____

_____

_____

_____

_____

_____

Notes:

Today's

Prayer of Faith

Father God, I commit to live my life by faith. Guide me into Your truth, and make me aware of it when I'm not responding in faith. In Jesus' Name. Amen.

Real-Life Testimonies
to Help Build Your Faith

He's No Halfway God

My little granddaughter, Kimber, at age 15 months, found some unscented lamp oil, swallowed some and vomited it up. It burned her lungs, and the doctors didn't give her any chance to live.

My daughter lived about 10 minutes from the hospital, but we live farther away. I heard Brother Copeland say to call things that be not as though they were. So, I started thanking God for healing Kimber. I did this continually for the three-hour drive [to the hospital to see her]. Every time I would be tempted to panic, I would confess her healing, instead.

Kimber stayed on life support for three days and in intensive care for a week. It has been two years now, and an X-ray of her lungs last week was perfectly clear!

I give all the praise and honor to God. What a great Savior we have. He never does things halfway!

Reba
Alabama

Chapter Two
What Faith Is *Not*

The Force of Faith
by Kenneth Copeland

Faith is not the product of reason.

As you work through today's Morning Connection, and throughout the rest of your day—and even throughout this entire action plan—meditate on that statement and get it down into your spirit.

Faith is not something you can conjure up. It is not a New Age version of mind over matter.

Faith is simply believing God and taking Him at His WORD. Whatever He says He'll do in His WORD, He will do, regardless of what it looks like, what situations may arise, or what philosophies become popular. Faith says, "God's WORD is the only authority that matters."

In Matthew 16:6 Jesus told His men to beware of the leaven of the Pharisees. They could not understand what He meant, and He asked, "Why do you reason among yourselves?" They missed what He was saying by trying to figure it out mentally. They were reasoning.

Believers are not to be led by logic, or even by "good sense." I have had my "sense" changed around to where it is good, but what the world calls good sense is not good at all. It is *bad* sense corrupted by Satan, the god of this world. If you want to find out what God thinks, take what the world thinks and reverse it. For example, the world says, "Seeing is believing." God says, "Believing is seeing."

Logic is the product of reasoning through what you can hear, taste, see, feel and smell. Reasoning is based on the world's system, something perverted by Satan. Faith is the product of God's WORD revealed by His Spirit and is based on the success of our heavenly Father.

Unreasonable Circumstances

The ministry of Jesus was never governed by logic or reason. In Mark 5, Jairus fell at the feet of Jesus and said, "My little daughter lieth at the point of death…come and lay thy hands on her…and she shall live" (verse 23). Reason would have said, "I'm sorry. I wish there was something I could do." Reason operates under the handicap of having no answer to critical needs. The request of this man was *un*reasonable, but Jesus answered him not a word and started toward his house.

On the way to Jairus' house, He met another unreasonable person—the little woman with the issue of blood. She had been to many physicians, but continued to grow worse. The doctors had reasoned that she was sick, but their logic had no cure to stop the flow of blood. (Understand that I am not criticizing doctors. Doctors are fighting the same destroyer we are. They are operating in the realm of the physical; we are operating in the realm of the spirit. They treat disease; we go to the root of the problem and deal with the enemy who causes disease.)

This little woman said, "If I may touch but his clothes, I shall be whole" (verse 28). There is no logic in that, is there? It just doesn't make good sense. Reason would have answered, "Hey lady, what's the matter with you? There is a little girl dying down here. I have to go see her. Let go of My clothes."

If Jesus had been ruled by *common sense,* as most of the Church has been in the past, He would have said, "Folks, let's back off here a minute. We haven't had the morning devotion. We haven't sung hymn number 246 or 391. Nobody has taken up the offering yet. Turn loose of My clothes, lady, for goodness' sake! We can't fool with you now. After all, you have already been to the doctor, and he said there was no hope. What can *I* do for you? Go on." Common sense will keep you bound when it is time to act in faith on God's WORD!

Look at Jesus. He was not led by logic. He was not led by the mind. He stopped and asked, "Who touched me?" (verse 31). Power had gone out of Him to heal and dry up the issue of blood—not reasoning power, but *spiritual* power. He said, "Daughter, your faith has made you whole." Her faith caused the power of God to flow into her body and make her whole. That healing was not the product of reason but the product of faith.

Common-sense religion will tell you not to get your hopes up. "God heals some people, but it might not be His will to heal you." That sounds *reasonable,* but it never gets results. You will always be the one whom it is not His will to heal. This approach to healing will not work because it is contrary to what The WORD of God says.

We are talking about being led by the Spirit, not by the common-sense world, not by the logical world. The Holy Spirit will turn you in the opposite direction from the way the world is going but, thank God, He *will* lead you in the direction God is going.

All you have to do is be like old Jairus. He didn't care what anyone thought. In fact, when the man came and told him, "Your little daughter is dead" (verse 35), he didn't say a word. He had already said what he had to say: "Lay your hands on my daughter, and she will live" (verse 23). Jesus turned and said to him, "Just believe." Jairus refused to be moved by what he heard—his *sense* of hearing. There was someone giving him the news that his daughter was dead, but in his heart there was a presence of a power stronger than the bad report. Something in his heart was saying, *I don't care what they say. This is so. I know it is so. I just know what I know! I refuse to give up.* That *something* in his heart was *faith.*

The Force of Faith

What was controlling the ministry of Jesus? The force of *faith.* And it was not entirely the force of His own faith. His own faith responded to the faith of the people. (It still does.)

In Nazareth He could do no mighty works because of unbelief (Mark 10). The people refused to believe. But on the other hand, the little woman's faith stopped Him in His tracks. Jairus' faith moved Him, and Jesus used His faith to raise Jairus' little girl. What was the result of Jairus' faith? He received his daughter back again from the dead. Unreasonable! Illogical! But that is victory of the highest order.

When you need more than just common-sense results, faith is the only way you will get them.

The Bible does not say, "Come, let us reason together, men." It does say, "Come now, and let us reason together, saith The LORD" (Isaiah 1:18). Reasoning with God is different than reasoning with men. God says, "Trust in The LORD with all thine heart; and lean not unto thine own understanding" (Proverbs 3:5). When men reason together, it is based on fear. Reasoning outside The WORD is always based on fear. Reasoning from men's minds, men's emotions and men's feelings is determined by fear because the world we live in is operating on the force of fear.

The LORD spoke to me once and said, *The definition of reasoning outside The WORD is "worry."* When you begin to reason outside God's WORD, you automatically begin to worry.

"What if that happens?" "What are we going to do if the Holy Ghost does break out in our denomination and people start talking in tongues right in the middle of church?" "What am I going to do?" The big *I*. That is selfishness. The root of selfishness is fear, not faith.

As we begin this journey into faith, settle it in your heart that faith is not the product of reason but of the reborn human spirit. It's not the product of the mind but of the heart. Faith is a power force. It is a tangible, conductive force. It will move things. Faith will change things. Faith will change the human body. It will change the human mind and heart. Faith will change your circumstances.

Morning Reflection

How does God's faith differ from the world's "faith"?

_____

_____

_____

_____

_____

Have you underdeveloped your faith because of reason or common sense? How?

_____

_____

_____

_____

_____

What can you learn from Jairus' example? Is this different from the way you have related to The LORD in the past? How?

_____

_____

_____

_____

_____

_____

Today's
Connection Points

● **Faith That Can Move Mountains CD: "Let God Arise" (Track 2)**

Put your faith in the greatness of God's ability. Let it settle into your spirit, and watch it change your circumstances!

● **DVD: "Faith Changes Everything" (Chapter 2)**

Gloria teaches you to keep your faith strong by keeping your eyes on Jesus, the author and finisher of your faith, and on His WORD. In Him, there are no limits to what your faith can do!

● **Faith Scriptures CD (Track 2)**

Mark 5:21-36, 6:5; Proverbs 3:5-6; Romans 5:1-2; Deuteronomy 28:1-2, 30:19-20

Faith
in Action

Whatever you're believing God for today, examine your thoughts. Ask yourself whether or not you're operating in faith.

Change your thoughts, if necessary, to what The WORD says about your situation.

Notes:

_____

_____

_____

_____

_____

_____

_____

_____

_____

_____

_____

_____

_____

_____

_____

_____

_____

_____

Faith Gives God an Opening
by Gloria Copeland

Everything that happens to us supernaturally happens by faith. Somewhere, somehow, someone has to release faith for the supernatural to happen in our lives. Just think for a moment how you came to be born again.

Maybe it was a friend, sibling or spouse who prayed for you to come into the kingdom of God. Maybe it was a great-great-grandmother who prayed for your salvation long before you were even born. It may have been someone on the other side of the world who interceded for you in the spirit, praying in other tongues and never even knowing what—or for whom—they prayed.

Oftentimes, we'll never know. But at some moment in time, faith must be released on our behalf for a supernatural event—like salvation—to happen.

In my life, I know of at least one person who prayed and released faith on my behalf concerning my salvation, but I didn't know it at the time. That person was Ken's mother. In fact, just a few months after Ken and I married, I got saved by reading a Bible that his mother had sent him for his birthday. It wasn't long afterward that Ken was born again, too.

So, whether it's getting us born again or healed, whether it's avoiding a financial disaster or avoiding a fatal car wreck, faith must be released. Someone's faith must be in operation—and if it's not our faith that gets us in the right place at the right time, then it's someone else's that does.

Isn't it comforting to know that God has people of faith and people of prayer scattered throughout each generation—people who pray and believe on our behalf?

But, you know, I discovered that you and I cannot live on someone else's faith the rest of our lives. If we try to, we probably won't live out the full number of our days on this earth. We won't walk in the fullness of the financial blessings God has stored up for us. We won't walk in the fullness of the ministry gifts God wants to pour out on us for the benefit of the world around us, a world that's full of lost, sick, lonely and needy people.

If you and I continue to depend only on the faith of other believers—our spouses, parents, children, or even our pastors and spiritual leaders—we will always be hindered and hampered, and never as free and successful as God wants us to be.

So we must develop our faith and learn how to operate in it.

Access to Favor

There are many principles to faith, but I want to introduce an important one to you: *Faith gives God an opening.*

We read in Romans 5:1-2, "Therefore being justified by faith, we have peace with God through our LORD Jesus Christ: By whom also we have access by faith into this grace wherein we stand, and rejoice in hope of the glory of God."

Verse 2 tells us we have "access," by faith, to the grace of God through our LORD Jesus, the Anointed One. It is our faith that allows us access to God's grace. That sounds reassuring, but what exactly does it mean?

Let's look at verse 2 in *The Amplified Bible:* "Through Him also we have [our] access (entrance, introduction) by faith into this grace—state of God's favor—in which we [firmly and safely] stand."

That's a mouthful, but basically, the Apostle Paul is telling us that faith gives us access to God's favor. Our faith gives God an opening through which He can pour all His favor into our lives.

The moment you and I received Jesus as our LORD, we gave God an opening into our lives. Our faith gave Him entrance to come in and save us. By faith, we gained access to the favor of God to be born again, but that was just the beginning.

There is still much more of God's favor for us to receive and experience every day of our lives. Faith requires that we continually receive The WORD of God to lay hold of all God's goodness. Faith is kept alive and working by taking God's WORD into our hearts.

Believing God's WORD concerning any area of life and acting in line with that WORD is faith. You and I were created by God with the ability to choose. He gave us a will. So, when it comes to our relating to and interacting with God, we make choices to believe what He says or not. Many times, the right choice requires faith to believe what He says rather than how it looks to the natural eye.

The Choice Is Yours

In Deuteronomy 28, as God prepared to cut covenant with His people, Israel, He told Moses to tell them, "And it shall come to pass, if thou shalt hearken [listen] diligently unto the voice of The LORD thy God, to observe and to do all his commandments which I command thee this day, that The LORD thy God will set thee on high above all nations of the earth: And all these blessings shall come on thee, and overtake thee..." (verses 1-2). That was the bright side of the picture.

On the other side, God warned Moses that if the people of Israel chose *not* to hearken [listen] to His voice and obey His commandments, then they would suffer consequences. The rest of Deuteronomy 28 contains more than 50 verses detailing the curses, already in the earth through Adam's treason, that would overtake them if they got out from under His covering.

God laid everything out for the Israelites—all the terms and details of His covenant. Then, He told them in Deuteronomy 30:19-20:

> I call heaven and earth to record this day against you, that I have set before you life and death, blessing and cursing: therefore choose life, that both thou and thy seed may live: That thou mayest love The LORD thy God, and that thou mayest obey his voice, and that thou mayest cleave unto him: for he is thy life, and the length of thy days: that thou mayest dwell in the land which The LORD sware unto thy fathers, to Abraham, to Isaac, and to Jacob, to give them.

The bottom line was whether or not the children of Israel trusted God enough to agree to His terms of the covenant. If they did, they would have to walk in His ways. They had to choose by faith.

A Choice to Make

Noah is a good example. When God first approached Noah about building the Ark, no one had ever heard of the concept of rain. No one knew drops of water could fall from the sky because it had never rained before. Up to that point, an underground sprinkler system of sorts—dew—had been used to water the earth. Yet, here was God talking to Noah about rain, floods and building a big boat.

Noah had a choice to make: *Do I believe God and build this monstrosity called an Ark, or don't I?* It was a far-out plan to Noah's natural understanding, but God knew exactly what He was doing.

Noah chose to believe God.

Once Noah made his decision, it took a long time to build that Ark. After all, he only had his family to help him build it. Everyone else thought he was crazy. "Crazy old Noah—building a floating house with no water to put it in."

Don't you know during the construction phase of that Ark, Noah had plenty of opportunities to change his mind and back out of that foolish-looking project of his? Nonetheless, he continued in faith. When God said: "Everything that is on the land shall die. But I will establish my covenant (promise, pledge) with you" (Genesis 6:17-18, *The Amplified Bible)*—Noah believed Him.

We find out that not only did Noah obey God by building the Ark, he also obeyed by preaching to the unrighteous people while he and his family hammered and sawed. He preached what God told him to preach. The Bible says Noah was a preacher of righteousness. I have no doubt the people said he was a "faith preacher"!

So, like Noah—and all the other heroes of faith in the Old Testament—if you and I are going to live supernaturally, and have the supernatural blessings of God overtake us, instead of curses, then we must give God an opening—and faith is that opening. Our faith is like opening a window to God.

Evening
Reflection

How does faith give God an opening?

_____

_____

_____

_____

How are obedience and faith tied together?

_____

_____

_____

_____

What is the Holy Spirit speaking to you through this evening's connection?

_____

_____

_____

_____

Notes:

_____

_____

_____

_____

_____

_____

_____

_____

_____

_____

_____

_____

_____

_____

_____

_____

_____

_____

_____

_____

_____

_____

_____

_____

_____

_____

_____

_____

_____

Today's Prayer of Faith

Father, I trust You with my whole heart. I don't lean to my own under-standing, but I choose to put my faith in You, knowing You always keep Your WORD. You are faithful! In Jesus' Name. Amen.

Real-Life Testimonies
to Help Build Your Faith

8-Year-Old Makes Lifetime Investment

When our children receive money for birthdays and Christmas, we usually have them put it in their bank accounts. This year, however, we allowed our older son Seth to keep a portion of his.

He decided to give $27 as an offering at church. He had heard of naming his seed, so he believed God for more money to put into the gospel. Seth planted his seed in December, and in March, on a Sunday after church, our pastor came and said someone had given him something for Seth. Our pastor put into Seth's hands five $20 bills! That's a lot of money for an 8-year-old!

He asked God what to do with the money, and God said to sow it back into His work. So, he decided to plant it into different ministries.

God honored His WORD and the faith of a child!

The Killian Family
N.C.

Chapter Three
You Have Faith

Yes, You Have Faith!
by Kenneth Copeland

"For by grace are ye saved through faith; and that not of yourselves: it is the gift of God" (Ephesians 2:8).

Everything in that verse is a gift from God. The grace is a gift from God, the salvation is a gift from God, and the faith to receive salvation is a gift from God. You can't create the faith the Apostle Paul was talking about here because it's not from you. This faith—the faith we're talking about in this Lifeline Kit—is from God alone.

"For I say, through the grace given unto me, to every man that is among you, not to think of himself more highly than he ought to think; but to think soberly, according as God hath dealt to every man the measure of faith" (Romans 12:3). Men have quoted this verse and said every man on earth has faith, but this scripture places a qualification on this measure of faith. Read it again: "For I say, through the grace given unto me, to every man that is among you."

Who was the Apostle Paul talking to? He was not talking to everyone in Rome. His letter was written to Christians.

Second Thessalonians 3:2 simply says, "…for all men have not faith." Not every man in the world has the God-kind of faith, but every *born-again* man does. Every child of God has world-overcoming faith.

The God-Kind of Faith

God's faith that the Bible mentions is imparted to you by your heavenly Father and resides within your spirit. It is in there to be developed and used in your daily life. Galatians 3:11 says we are to live by it: "The just shall live by faith." God has given you this powerful faith to sustain you in this life. It is so powerful, even a measure as big as a mustard seed can pluck up a mountain and throw it into the sea (Mark 11:23).

Every person who has received the new birth, or been born again, and made Jesus The LORD of his life, has had this faith put inside him. You could not have been born again without it.

Listen to me—*you have faith!*

For you to say or believe, "I don't have enough faith," or "I don't have any faith," is a slap in the face of The WORD of God. Hebrews 12:2 says Jesus is the author and finisher of your faith. This faith is good enough to make all things possible to you, the believer (Mark 9:23).

Let's make absolutely certain that what we have said agrees with The WORD. Remember, we have said that faith is born in the human heart at the time of conversion. So, every born-again believer has the faith of God in him, *now.* We have said that the measure of faith in the heart of the believer is enough to do whatever it is called upon to do. Jesus is the author of our faith. Look at 1 John 5:1-5:

Whosoever believeth that Jesus is the Christ is born of God: and every one that loveth him that begat loveth him also that is begotten of him. By this we know that we love the children of God, when we love God, and keep his commandments. For this is the love of God, that we keep his commandments: and his commandments are not grievous. For whatsoever is born of God overcometh the world: and this is the victory that overcometh the world, even our faith. Who is he that overcometh the world, but he that believeth that Jesus is the Son of God?

These verses tell us whosoever believes that Jesus is the Christ has enough victory faith in him to overcome the world. Just so there is no mistake about it, verse 5 asks the question: "Who is he that overcometh the world, but he that believeth that Jesus is the Son of God?" The power used to overcome the world is our faith. Think of it! There is enough of God's very own faith residing on the inside of you right now to overcome anything the world can throw at you!

God is a faith being. You are born of Him, so *you* are a faith being. God does not do anything outside of faith. With His faith living in you, you are to operate the same way.

How do you know you have faith?

_____

_____

_____

_____

What can even a mustard seed-sized amount of faith do? What does this mean for your situation?

_____

_____

_____

_____

How can you begin to act on your faith? Be specific.

_____

_____

_____

_____

Today's
Connection Points

● *Faith That Can Move Mountains* CD: "Nothing Is Impossible" (Track 3)

Nothing is impossible for the one who is living by faith in God!

● DVD: "You Have His Faith" (Chapter 3)

There is nothing that faith can't overcome. It's Jesus' own overcoming faith in you, bringing you through to victory!

● *Faith Scriptures* CD (Track 3)

Ephesians 2:8; Romans 12:3; Galatians 3:11; Mark 11:20-24; Hebrews 12:2; 1 John 5:1-5; Romans 10:13-17; 2 Corinthians 1:20

Faith
in Action

You have faith—not just any faith, but the God-kind of faith inside you.
Begin to live with the confidence that you are a faith being!

Notes:

_____

_____

_____

_____

_____

_____

_____

_____

_____

_____

_____

_____

_____

_____

_____

_____

_____

_____

Faith Comes by Listening
by Gloria Copeland

God is no dictator. He never forces His way into our lives like the devil does. He never tries to deceive us. When God laid out His promises, He made them plain and simple. Then, He gave us a choice.

Certainly, you and I don't have to believe what God says. But if we want to live healed, prosperous and blessed in every way, then we will have to believe what He says. That's faith!

Psalm 35:27 says God "hath pleasure in the prosperity of his servant." But that doesn't mean we have to walk in prosperity. If we want to, we can live in the natural realm and refuse supernatural increase. God won't force it on us.

If, however, we choose to take God at His WORD, we can walk in the fullness of His prosperity for our lives. All we have to do is give Him an opening. All we have to do is believe what He says, instead of believing what we see, hear or feel.

This is so important to understand: *Faith comes.*

Like God, faith is no respecter of persons. Ken shared with you this morning about how God has given you faith. Remember, Romans 12:3, which was spoken to born-again believers, tells us that God "hath dealt to every man the measure of faith."

Likewise, every believer can *develop* their faith. Faith will always come when God's WORD is heard and received. It happened when you first heard the gospel and were saved: "For whosoever shall call upon the name of The LORD shall be saved" (Romans 10:13).

But read on, and you'll see what causes faith to rise up in any situation:

For whosoever shall call upon the name of The LORD shall be saved. How then shall they call on him in whom they have not believed? and how shall they believe in him of whom they have not heard? and how shall they hear without a preacher? And how shall they preach, except they be sent? as it is written, How beautiful are the feet of them that preach the gospel of peace, and bring glad tidings of good things! But they have not all obeyed the gospel. For Esaias saith, LORD, who hath believed our report? So then faith cometh by hearing, and hearing by The WORD of God (verses 13-17).

First, Paul declares a promise from God—"Whosoever shall call upon the name of The LORD shall be saved" (verse 13). Then, he goes on to show the supernatural process by which it draws faith out of our hearts—the faith that is necessary to lay hold of the promise and cause the reality of it to manifest in our lives.

Faith Comes by Hearing

This is just one of approximately 6,000 promises from God recorded in the Bible, and each one was carefully written down for us.

If you and I were to take each of those promises and read them, speak them out loud and keep them before our eyes, in our mouths and in our ears—eventually—faith would rise up within us. Why? Because faith comes by hearing The WORD of God. Faith comes by hearing the promises of God.

Faith is simply believing what we hear in God's WORD. It's believing what we read and what we say from God's WORD. If we believe what we hear, say and read, and let it get deep into our hearts, soon faith will rise up within us and see to it that those things come to pass. The faith that rises within us gives God an opening to bring His promises to pass.

This point is reinforced—though in a negative sense—by Paul's account of what Isaiah had to say about the unbelieving children of Israel.

"LORD, who hath believed our report?" (Romans 10:16).

The Israelites of old really did not believe God's promises. They didn't take His covenant to heart. How do we know they didn't? We just read in verse 16 that they didn't obey the gospel. Because they did not take God's WORD to heart, faith didn't rise within them.

To illustrate this point, let's say I were to tell Kenneth, "You know, I noticed you were excited about that Harley motorcycle you saw for sale the other day, and I've been thinking and praying about it, and I just want to bless you with it. I want to buy that motorcycle for you."

If I were to make a promise like that to Kenneth, and he knew I would keep my word, and knew I had the money to buy it, I guarantee you he would get excited. Why?

Based on my word, resources and promise, Kenneth would have faith that I would do what I said. In fact, I'm confident he'd start acting as though he already had the keys to that motorcycle in his hand.

He'd start thinking about where he could go on his new motorcycle and what other pieces of chrome and pinstripes he could put on it. He would be in an absolute stir over my promise to buy him a new motorcycle. He would already see himself riding it.

Well, it's no different with God. If God promises He will do something, He will do it. He is more dependable than anyone you know.

Remember those 6,000 promises recorded in the Bible?

They've already been established as reality for us. We read in 2 Corinthians 1:20 that "all the promises of God in [Jesus] are yea, and in [Jesus] Amen."

So, if you need healing, it's done. If you need food, it's done. If you need protection, it's done. If you need a house or a job, it's done. You and I don't have to try and talk God into any of these things—they're already done! God promised them to us. Then, He ratified His promise through the blood of Jesus, the sacrifice of His own Son.

You and I must keep the promises of God—His precious words—before us at all times... reading them, speaking them, listening to them. In short, we must do everything it takes to get His WORD into our hearts. Because when we do...faith *will* come!

Memorize this: "So then faith cometh by hearing, and hearing by The WORD of God" (Romans 10:17).

We're going to look at this in even more depth tomorrow because I want you to commit to God's WORD. Commit to it, and I guarantee that faith won't just come some of the time or, maybe, most of the time. No, faith *will* come *all the time!* It will come every time you believe it enough to receive it into your heart to abide. And, when it comes, so will the fulfillment of God's promises in your life!

Evening Reflection

What causes your faith to rise up?

_____
_____
_____
_____
_____

How do you know God will keep His promises to you?

_____
_____
_____
_____
_____

How do you give God an opening into your life?

_____
_____
_____
_____
_____

Notes:

_____
_____
_____
_____
_____
_____
_____
_____
_____
_____
_____
_____

Today's Prayer of Faith

Father, in the Name of Jesus, I commit to believe Your WORD and obey the leading of Your Holy Spirit. I confess that my faith is growing stronger every day as I saturate myself in Your WORD. I thank You that as I make the quality decision to walk in faith in Your WORD, I will receive what Your WORD promises me. Amen!

Real-Life Testimonies
to Help Build Your Faith

A Match Made in Heaven

I would like to praise God, and thank you for standing with me. The LORD brought me a marriage partner—the man I had prayed for. The LORD had me focus on a couple featured in a recent *Believer's Voice of Victory* magazine, and to speak in faith that that would be my story, too.

I met Stephen on Christmas Day and we married the following June. God was in the relationship from the beginning. We both commented on the extreme peace we experienced during courtship, and God even gave us the date for our wedding. THE BLESSING was present throughout the service. There was an atmosphere of great rejoicing and worship, and two people received Jesus during the ceremony. God is so good, I praise His holy Name!

Carole and Stephen
Pennsylvania

Chapter Four
Our Source of Faith

The WORD Source
by Kenneth Copeland

Let's begin today with the verse Gloria ended with yesterday: "So then faith cometh by hearing, and hearing by The WORD of God" (Romans 10:17).

The WORD of God produces faith in your heart. There is no other source for it. Get that? There is *no* other way to build your faith than with, through and by The WORD of God. Anything else is just a mental exercise. The more WORD you hear and put into your heart, the more your faith is developed. Period.

Your confession—or the words you speak—reflect the level of The WORD of God that is working in you. When you are filled with God's WORD, faith comes up strong. When you neglect your study and meditation time and take on the cares of this life, you stop the force of faith from coming out of your spirit. If you want to live successfully in your Christian walk, then you must—*must*—feed your spirit The WORD of God.

> My son, attend to my words; incline thine ear unto my sayings. Let them not depart from thine eyes; keep them in the midst of thine heart. For they are life unto those that find them, and health to all their flesh. Keep thy heart with all diligence; for out of it are the issues of life (Proverbs 4:20-23).

The force of faith that comes from The WORD in your heart brings life and health to your flesh. The WORD not only brings healing, it keeps you healthy. Above all that you do, diligently protect and nourish your spirit. Feed your heart with God's WORD, and the force of faith will issue out of it and work whenever it is needed.

Faith, like any other force, must be applied in order to gain any benefit from it. As we eat physical food, our bodies turn that food into strength. The strength in the body, then, must be applied. It must be released. It must be activated. The same is true with faith. The spirit man consumes spiritual food—God's WORD—and that spiritual food produces spiritual power—faith. Faith is released two ways: by our words and our actions. Jesus said in John 3:21, "He that doeth truth cometh to the light, that his deeds may be made manifest, that they are wrought in God." James 2:17 says, "Even so faith, if it hath not works, is dead." One translation says, "Faith without corresponding action will not work."

Begin putting God's WORD in your heart. As an act of your will, believe it. Say it with your mouth and act accordingly. The WORD tells us our God meets our needs according to His riches in glory by Christ Jesus (Philippians 4:19). Begin to talk as though that's true—because it is! This is faith receiving what God has already provided for us in Christ Jesus. Praise God! It is already ours. We must release our faith in The WORD and talk and act like that WORD is true. Then, we will see the desired results.

Hearing and Speaking

Read Romans 10:17 again: "So then faith cometh by hearing, and hearing by The WORD of God." We're going to study the importance of your words later in this LifeLine Kit, but I would be doing you a disservice if I didn't address it here, also. The words you speak are key to applying your faith. When you put faith-filled words—God's WORD—into your heart, faith-filled words come out of your mouth.

Faith is the product of your spirit. It comes into your spirit by hearing The WORD, and it is continually developed in your spirit by The WORD.

Faith's results are determined by your confession, or what you say. Your confession corresponds to the level of The WORD of God that is working in you. When you are filled with God's WORD, faith comes up strong. Slacking off in your study and meditation time opens the door for you to become caught up in the affairs of life and consumes or uses up the force of faith coming out of your spirit.

Taking Action

Jesus said, "The words that I speak unto you, they are spirit, and they are life" (John 6:63). Read that again. The words that Jesus spoke—The WORD of God—are *life!*

Begin by putting God's WORD into your heart. As an act of your will, believe it on purpose. Then, say it with your mouth and act accordingly.

The Bible says God is your strength (Psalm 46:1). So, begin to talk and act strong—even before you feel strong or look strong.

The Bible says you are healed (1 Peter 2:24). Begin to talk healed and to act healed.

The Bible says that God meets your needs according to His riches in glory (Philippians 4:19). Begin to talk as though it were true because *it is true!* This is faith receiving what God has already provided for us in Jesus.

Learn and develop this confession of faith: "I am not moved by what I see or by what I feel. I am moved only by what I believe. I believe The WORD of God. The victory is mine! I have it *now!* I can see it through the eyes of my faith!"

Continually return to The WORD of God. It is the source for your spiritual and physical health. Everything in your life needs to be based on it in order to succeed. So, get to it—get to reading, get to confessing, get to living The WORD-based life!

Morning
Reflection

What is the source of faith?

_____

_____

_____

_____

How is your faith affected by what you say or do?

_____

_____

_____

_____

Why must you apply your faith in order to benefit from it?

_____

_____

_____

_____

Today's
Connection Points

- **Faith That Can Move Mountains CD: "In Christ Alone" (Track 4)**

  As you go about your day today, keep your eyes fixed on Jesus, the Anointed One and His Anointing, and His WORD!

- **DVD: "The WORD Brings Faith" (Chapter 4)**

  Learn about the exciting life of faith! It's easy to put God's WORD first place in your life when you see that the more you learn, the more your needs are met, the freer you are and the more wonderful life becomes!

- **Faith Scriptures CD (Track 4)**

  Romans 10:17; Proverbs 4:20-23; James 2:17; John 6:63; Hebrews 4:12, _The Amplified Bible;_ Isaiah 55:10-11, _The Amplified Bible;_ Joshua 1:7-8, _The Amplified Bible;_ Proverbs 6:20-22

Faith in Action

Make a quality decision to read and meditate on The WORD of God.

Begin speaking and acting as though the things you are believing for have already occurred.

Notes:

Let The WORD Abide in You
by Gloria Copeland

For years, I prayed without getting any sort of answer. I didn't know what it took to pray effectively, and because of that, most of my prayers were just a rehearsal of the problem.

But God already knew the problem! What He needed was for me to open the door of faith, so He could move into my life and *solve* that problem. But I had weak faith. I didn't believe I received when I prayed according to Mark 11:24.

So what happened as a result of those faithless prayers? For the most part, nothing at all. "But Gloria," you ask, "couldn't you have prayed for more faith?"

Yes, I could have, but I wouldn't have received any that way because faith doesn't come by praying. As we've been studying, it comes by hearing The WORD of God. The only way you can obtain faith is to hear The WORD preached or take it into yourself by spending time in it!

Of course, you can spend a lifetime studying The WORD like a textbook, just to gain natural knowledge, or to learn facts, but it won't generate faith or do anything else for you spiritually. For The WORD to be effective in your life, you have to let it become more than just a book to you. You must treat it as though God is speaking to you, personally, through its pages. You must let God's words jump out of your Bible and into your heart, so they can *abide,* or take up residence there.

God's words can do that because they're not just tired, dead, old phrases. They are supernatural words that originated in heaven. As Hebrews 4:12 says:

> The WORD that God speaks is alive and full of power [making it active, operative, energizing, and effective]; it is sharper than any two-edged sword, penetrating to the dividing line of the breath of life (soul) and [the immortal] spirit, and of joints and marrow [of the deepest parts of our nature], exposing and sifting and analyzing and judging the very thoughts and purposes of the heart *(The Amplified Bible).*

God's words had life in them the moment He first spoke them. And, even though they've been written in a Book for thousands of years, those words are still as powerful and full of life as they were the day God said them. His words are eternal. Jesus said they are spirit and they are life (John 6:63). So, when you take the words in that Book and put them into your heart and into your mouth, they bring supernatural things to pass.

God's WORD makes a circle. It comes down to us from Him like rain from heaven and goes into the soil of our hearts (Mark 4). Then, we lift those words back up to Him by faith, in prayer, and He brings them to pass in our lives.

Isaiah 55:10-11 says it like this:

As the rain and snow come down from the heavens, and return not there again, but water the earth and make it bring forth and sprout, that it may give seed to the sower and bread to the eater, So shall My WORD be that goes forth out of My mouth: it shall not return to Me void [without producing any effect, useless], but it shall accomplish that which I please and purpose, and it shall prosper in the thing for which I sent it *(The Amplified Bible).*

Keep The WORD Alive in You

Remember though, if you want The WORD to produce those kinds of powerful results in your life, you can't be content just to "know" it. You must believe it and meditate on it until it abides in you, and you'll obey it. You must give your attention to it just as God instructed Joshua to do in Joshua 1. You must:

Turn not from it to the right hand or to the left, that you may prosper wherever you go. This book...shall not depart out of your mouth, but you shall meditate on it day and night, that you may observe and do according to all that is written in it. For then you shall make your way prosperous, and then you shall deal wisely and have good success (verses 7-8, *The Amplified Bible).*

I realize, of course, that you can't walk around reading your Bible 24 hours a day. But if you're committed to abiding in The WORD, you'll find ways to put it into your heart. You can certainly keep The WORD abiding in you 24 hours a day.

Ken and I first learned to walk by faith back in the 1960s by listening to 7-inch reel-to-reel tapes by Kenneth E. Hagin. (It's so much easier today!)

Every day I'd hurry and finish my housework so I could sit down and listen to those tapes. I listened to them so many times and took so many notes, I eventually wrote down, word for word, a great part of those tapes. I still have my notebook.

In addition, whenever Brother Hagin held a meeting there in Tulsa, we found a way to be there. I believe, in the year we lived there, he held four 10-day meetings, and we didn't miss one of them. We had to slip and slide our way over ice-covered streets to attend some of them, but we did it because we were so desperate for The WORD!

That desperation paid off, too. Before long, things in our lives began to change. Because we started abiding in The WORD, The WORD started abiding in us.

How do you know if The WORD is abiding in you? It begins to speak to you. If The WORD is not talking to you, then it's not alive in you, and you need to freshen your remembrance of it. Proverbs 6:20-22 says:

My son, keep thy father's commandment, and forsake not the law of thy mother: Bind them continually upon thine heart, and tie them about thy neck. When thou goest, it shall lead thee...and when thou awakest, it shall talk with thee.

The WORD that's abiding in you, The WORD that's alive in you, is The WORD that talks to you. It's The WORD that leads you moment by moment as you go about your day. The abiding WORD will come up in your heart unexpectedly, much like the words and notes of a familiar song might waft spontaneously through your mind.

To conquer the challenges of the devil, you must have the spiritual strength within you that only the engrafted WORD can provide. You have to be so established in that WORD that it automatically rises up within you at the moment of crisis.

No Deposit/No Return

If The WORD is not abiding in you as it should, if it's not coming up inside you when you need it, the solution is simple. Spend more time in it. Put more of The WORD in your heart...and more will come out!

In some ways, your heart is like a bank account. If you want to write faith checks on that account, you must have plenty of WORD in there to back them. Jesus said, "A good man brings good things out of the good stored up in him, and an evil man brings evil things out of the evil stored up in him" (Matthew 12:33-35, *New International Version*).

If you haven't put money in the bank, when you write a check, money will not come out of the bank. The WORD is the same way. If you haven't deposited God's WORD about healing into your heart, when you become sick, words of healing will not come out of your mouth. If you haven't deposited God's WORD about prosperity in your heart, when the devil attacks your finances, you won't have the spiritual funds to fight back.

"But, I did deposit God's WORD about healing in my heart," you say. "I read healing scriptures every day, back in 1990."

You probably deposited a thousand dollars in the bank a few years ago, too—but are you living on that money today? Of course not! It's long gone. You cashed checks on it and used it all.

By the same token, in this life, you have to walk by faith, so you are continually writing faith checks. The WORD you put inside you is made strength and produces faith (if you believe it and keep it), and you're continually drawing on that supply of strength to meet the challenges that come your way. You are always encountering situations that require supernatural help. So, to keep your strength account from running low, you must continually make deposits of The WORD. You must keep a fresh deposit of The WORD in your heart at all times by putting it in daily.

Right now, you may not be in a position to make huge deposits of money into your natural bank account. But you can make any size deposit you want to make in your heart account—and that's the account that really matters—because it's the one you must draw on to change the circumstances in your life. It holds the faith you'll need to cover any bill the devil tries to send your way.

When you're first starting your faith account, it's wise to begin making deposits in the area of your greatest need. If your biggest problem is finances, for example, you should set your attention on The WORD of God concerning prosperity. You ought to go to The WORD and start the power of God working in you, so faith will rise up in your heart and cause you to prosper.

So, give Him an opportunity! Open the door of faith for Him by spending time in His WORD. Meditate on it until that WORD becomes bigger inside you than the circumstances that surround you. Set your attention on The WORD that gives you an answer to the problem you're facing. Then, focus on God's answer until you can look right past the circumstances and into the realm of the spirit. Focus on it until you can see God's WORD coming to pass for you!

When you do that, you'll find that poverty and lack, sickness and failure of every kind will wither. They will lose their energy to stay in your life, and the provision of God will gain energy and bring you what you need.

By building your faith account, you'll bankrupt the devil in your life. He just won't have the resources to keep you down anymore. If he tries to put sickness on you, you can draw on The WORD of God about healing, and it will give you victory in that area.

But remember, you can't make a withdrawal from an account that doesn't have anything in it. No deposit, no return!

If you need more faith in your heart to meet the challenges you're facing right now, put some in there. Since faith comes by hearing The WORD, you can have as much as you want. The amount of WORD you put in your heart is how much faith you will have.

But, remember this: No one can make deposits into your heart account but you. Your spouse can't do it for you. Your pastor can't do it for you. Even God can't do it for you. You're the one who has to open your Bible every day. You're the one who has to listen to that teaching series, go to that meeting where The WORD is being preached and attend that church where The WORD is being preached. You're the one who has to open your ears and your heart and receive the living WORD!

From the first day Ken and I began to walk by faith, our lives began to improve. But, breakthrough didn't manifest overnight. It took time. It took a while for us to lay hold of The WORD of God to such an extent that it could significantly change our circumstances. It took time for The WORD to work its way down into our hearts and take root there, to take over our minds and mouths, and then become fruitful.

So, don't become impatient. Don't expect to revolutionize your entire life in a day or two. Give The WORD time to work. Your life will never be the same!

Evening Reflection

How is God's WORD alive?

_____

_____

_____

_____

How can you keep The WORD in your heart 24 hours a day?

_____

_____

_____

_____

How is your heart like a bank account?

_____

_____

_____

_____

_____

_____

_____

Notes:

Today's
Prayer of Faith

Father, I make a commitment today to give Your WORD first place in my life. I will put it into my heart continually—and I know it will spring up as faith! Thank You, LORD, that just as Proverbs 6:22 says, Your WORD will rise in my heart, come to my mind and lead me. In Jesus' Name. Amen.

Real-Life Testimonies
to Help Build Your Faith

God Said It—I Believe It

I caught a cold, had a complication in my left ear and ended up having only 30 percent of my hearing. I was only 40 years old, but doctors told me the hearing loss could not be restored, and that I had to take treatment to stop more hearing loss. I had no money and no work at the time, so I accepted the thought that I would live without hearing in my left ear.

But, when I listened to Kenneth and Gloria's sermons, I was surprised at the fact that people were healed. Then, I started calling things that are not as though they were. I started praying and believing God that I have 100 percent of my hearing.

This year, I passed all medical examinations, and I can hear with my left ear!

V.P.
Ukraine

Chapter Five
Faith-Filled Words

Faith-Filled Words

by Kenneth Copeland

And Jesus answering saith unto them, Have faith in God. For verily I say unto you, That whosoever shall say unto this mountain, Be thou removed, and be thou cast into the sea; and shall not doubt in his heart, but shall believe that those things which he saith shall come to pass; he shall have whatsoever he saith (Mark 11:22-23).

In today's language, this account would read something like this: "Jesus spoke to the mountain, and it was gone." In explaining it, Jesus said, "This is the way you operate the faith of God: You speak the desired result and do not doubt in your heart. You believe that your words have power, and the things you say will come to pass. The result is that you can have whatever you say when you believe."

Jesus said to believe that the *things* you say will come to pass. This doesn't mean you can continue to speak any way you want, and then in a time of need expect to exercise faith in God's words. If you really believe faith words, you should speak them all the time.

You must change your vocabulary and discipline your speech so your words are becoming to Jesus. *All* your words should be words of faith. You should only speak words you want to come to pass and believe they will produce results. By getting into The WORD of God and continually feeding on it so faith controls your vocabulary, you can come to the place where all your words will come to pass. When your words are words of faith, God will be able to trust you with His power in the words of your mouth. What you speak, good or bad, is what you will receive.

Jesus said, "For out of the abundance of the heart the mouth speaketh" (Matthew 12:34). The force of faith must be behind your words for them to cause things to come to pass. *You must believe in your heart.* Your mouth will speak what is put into your heart. If faith-filled words are put into your heart, faith-filled words will come out. If doubt and unbelief are put into your heart, words of doubt and unbelief will come out. Words bring things to pass. Your words work for you or against you. They enforce the law of sin and death, or they enforce the law of the Spirit of life in Christ Jesus (Romans 8:2).

The force of faith, then, is released in words. Faith-filled words put the law of the Spirit of life into operation. Jesus said, "The thief cometh not, but for to steal, and to kill, and to destroy: I am come that they might have life, and that they might have it more abundantly" (John 10:10).

The abundant life Jesus mentioned is still freely offered. However, many Christians are not living it because of ignorance (Hosea 4:6).

Understanding the System

Once you learn how the system works, then you can see how Satan has been manipulating it for his own cause. James 3:6 says, "And the tongue is a fire, a world of iniquity...and [it] setteth on fire the course of nature; and it is set on fire of hell." From the moment you were born, you were trained to speak negatively about your life and your circumstances. By using your tongue, Satan sets in motion the course of nature in your life.

Stop and listen to your everyday conversation. Train yourself to hear your own words. Much of it is so-called "casual" remarks that you make, never thinking of the effect those words are having on your life.

For instance, when cold weather first sets in, there is much talk about the flu season being just around the corner. People comment to friends about the extra doctor bills they will have to pay. This kind of remark is a product of fear that sickness and disease is coming, that it's inevitable.

If asked, "Do you believe in healing?" you'd answer, "Yes, of course," but your everyday conversation may negate that statement of faith. Proverbs 6:2 says you are snared with the words of your mouth.

As you make statements of fear, doubt, unbelief, etc., the pilot light of destruction is lit, and Satan will fan the flame every way he can to make it grow. Then, once he gets that fire built up around you, he will attack. To your untrained eye, it will seem that tragedy struck from out of nowhere. The first thing you do is question, "Why? Why did this happen to me?" It seems to be an unanswerable question, but there is an answer: The tongue sets on fire the course of nature, and the tongue is set on fire by hell itself.

By knowing that your tongue controls the entire course of your life, you can put a stop to Satan's operation. Though it may seem impossible, it can be done, but it requires the power of the Holy Spirit at work in your life.

James 3:7-8 says, "For every kind of beasts, and of birds, and of serpents, and of things in the sea, is tamed, and hath been tamed of mankind: but the tongue can no man tame; it is an unruly evil, full of deadly poison." Man can tame the wild beasts, but he cannot tame his own tongue.

This does not say that the tongue cannot be tamed. It simply says that man cannot tame it. The tongue cannot be tamed with the same natural power that man uses to tame the animals. It takes spiritual power, and spiritual power is what every born-again believer has at his disposal. Jesus said, "My words are spirit" (John 6:63). Thank God for His written WORD!

Your tongue is only an instrument. Your heart is where the key lies. Whatever is in your heart is what will come out of your mouth. If you fill your heart with God's WORD, then God's WORD will come out of your mouth. You can begin today setting a new standard for your life by changing the words that come out of your mouth—words of life, words of power, words of faith!

Morning
Reflection

What do your words say? Do they match what God's WORD says?

_____

_____

_____

What do your words say about what you believe in your heart?

_____

_____

_____

How can you change what's in your heart?

_____

_____

_____

Today's
Connection Points

(•) *Faith That Can Move Mountains* CD: "Weakness for Strength" (Track 5)

Make the decision—on purpose—to trade your old way of thinking and speaking for God's way of doing things!

(•) DVD: "Speaking Faith" (Chapter 5)

Gloria teaches you how to activate your faith to receive what you need. Experience victory in *every* situation!

(•) *Faith Scriptures* CD (Track 5)

Mark 11:22-23; Matthew 12:34; Romans 8:2; John 10:10; Isaiah 55:10-11

Faith in Action

Think about your words over the past week.

Consider how they reflect what's really in your heart and how you can change them to bring forth the victory you desire in every area of your life!

Notes:

Faith Acts

by Gloria Copeland

God framed the worlds by faith. Everything God made, He made by faith. Everything He does, He does by faith.

For you and me, it's no different. What works for God will work for us.

But *how* did God make everything by faith? If we knew that, we could frame *our* worlds, too, right? Well, in Genesis 1, we find that God's faith was released with *words*.

The account of Creation goes something like this:

"In the beginning God said, Let there be light...and there was light. God said, Let there be a firmament...and it was so. God said, Let us make man...."

Do you see the pattern?

"God said...and it was so. God said...and it was so." God literally spoke all of Creation into existence. Hebrews 11:3 says that the worlds were framed by The WORD of God. That is the very same way we frame our worlds. We are created in God's image to live like Him!

Notice, that Genesis doesn't say "God thought...and it was so." No, God spoke. That's how He operates. That's how faith operates. What's more, God has never stopped speaking.

Down through the Old Testament and into the New, we see how God continued to pour His WORD into the earth, primarily using prophets to speak His WORD. The reason God released all that WORD into the earth was to give substance for when the time came for Jesus— the ultimate WORD given by God—to appear in the flesh. He brought Jesus into the earth by His WORD!

Get Your Mouth in Gear

I like to describe faith like this: Faith is movement. It's a mouth in motion.

Here's an example of what I mean.

Let's say my body is being attacked with symptoms of sickness.

Thousands of years ago, God spoke a promise about healing into the earth. He spoke through His prophet Isaiah and said: "Surely he hath borne our griefs [sickness, weakness and distress], and carried our sorrows: yet we did esteem him stricken, smitten of God, and afflicted. But he was wounded for our transgressions, he was bruised for our iniquities: the chastisement of our peace was upon him; and with his stripes we are healed" (Isaiah 53:4-5).

Many years after that prophecy was spoken, Jesus came—God's promise in the flesh— to fulfill that WORD. Galatians 3:13 describes the results of Jesus having come to this earth: "Christ hath redeemed us from the curse of the law, being made a curse for us: for it is written, Cursed is every one that hangeth on a tree."

Looking back on Jesus' ministry, the Apostle Peter also wrote, "Who his own self [Jesus] bare our sins in his own body on the tree, that we, being dead to sins, should live unto righteousness: by whose stripes ye WERE healed" (1 Peter 2:24).

Now, here I am with symptoms of sickness attacking my body. What do I do?

Remember, faith is what gives substance to that for which you and I hope. In this case, I'm hoping to be delivered from this sickness.

Faith also gives God the opening necessary for Him to pour His favor and blessing into our lives, bringing the manifestation of that promise, and its provisions, from the spiritual realm into the natural realm—which is where my body needs it at the moment.

But now, how does faith make that draw on God's WORD? By taking action.

And how does my faith take action? By speaking The WORD and then acting as though it is done. Romans 10:6-10 describes the process like this:

> But the righteousness which is of faith speaketh on this wise, Say not in thine heart, Who shall ascend into heaven? (that is, to bring Christ down from above:) Or, Who shall descend into the deep? (that is, to bring up Christ again from the dead.) But what saith it? The WORD is nigh thee, even in thy mouth, and in thy heart: that is, the word of faith, which we preach; That if thou shalt confess with thy mouth The LORD Jesus, and shalt believe in thine heart that God hath raised him from the dead, thou shalt be saved. For with the heart man believeth unto righteousness; and with the mouth confession is made unto salvation.

The provision for all that God has promised us—health, healing, salvation, protection, prosperity—has already been established in heaven and earth. The work was completed 2,000 years ago. Receiving that provision is up to us. That's where mouth and motion come into play.

In Isaiah 55:10-11, we read:

> For as the rain cometh down, and the snow from heaven, and returneth not thither, but watereth the earth, and maketh it bring forth and bud, that it may give seed to the sower, and bread to the eater: So shall my WORD be that goeth forth out of my mouth: it shall not return unto me void, but it shall accomplish that which I please, and it shall prosper in the thing whereto I sent it.

Our new hearts, like the earth, are good ground for The WORD of God. They are the abiding and functioning place for His WORD.

Likewise, our mouths are the implements of faith that speak the words out of our hearts to enable us to reap the harvest we desire. We reap that harvest by believing and thus speaking the promises of God into fulfillment. That's why we read in James 2:14, 17: "What doth it profit, my brethren, though a man say he hath faith, and have not works? can faith save him? Even so faith, if it hath not works, is dead, being alone."

Our faith must act. The faith stored in our hearts must come out. Otherwise, it is dead and of no use. You release faith with your words.

You and I have the responsibility of getting our hearts and mouths in gear, speaking and acting as though we've already received the fulfillment of our desire. We believe we receive when we pray. From the moment we release our faith, we must talk and act as though it is done. We must take action by speaking as God spoke and give substance to His promises. As we do, we give substance to something we can drive, something we can eat, something we can wear, something that can heal our bodies. We give substance to our world.

Evening Reflection

Why is faith heaven's window into our lives?

_____

_____

_____

How does your faith take action?

_____

_____

_____

How has God released His WORD into the earth? Why is this important?

_____

_____

_____

Notes:

_____

_____

_____

_____

_____

_____

_____

_____

_____

_____

_____

_____

_____

_____

_____

_____

_____

Today's Prayer of Faith

Father God, I thank You for Your WORD and for Your Son, Jesus. By faith, I receive all You have for me. As I deposit Your WORD into my heart, I will speak it out loud in faith, believing that it will accomplish Your perfect will in my life. In Jesus' Name. Amen.

Real-Life Testimonies
to Help Build Your Faith

Believe and Receive!

Thank you for your prayer of agreement for my husband. In spite of Alzheimer's disease, The LORD opened his mind to clearly understand and repeat from his heart the prayer of salvation. After 31 years of believing for his salvation, it came to pass!

As it is written in Mark 9:23: "All things are possible to him that believeth." Now, I stand in faith for our daughter, her husband, children and grandchildren. I am truly a blessed woman!

M.B.
Canada

Chapter Six
How Faith Works

Faith Works by Love
by Kenneth Copeland

As we continue learning about faith and how to live by faith, we must also learn about the love of God. The best place to start learning about it is 1 John.

John is called the "apostle of love." In the first chapter, verses 1-3, he explains the reason for his writing is to tell what the apostles had seen, heard and experienced when they were with Jesus, so we too, can have relationship with one another, with God the Father and with His Son, Jesus Christ. This is important because what he and the other apostles experienced with Jesus was a lesson in divine love.

Without a revelation of the love of God, you'll never have close fellowship and communion with Him and therefore never walk in faith to the fullest extent. There will always be an unwarranted fear of Him if you don't know and believe He loves you. You cannot live in fear of God and live by faith in Christ Jesus. The two are diametrically opposed.

So, let's begin today's Morning Connection by looking at 1 John 4:15-16: "Whosoever shall confess that Jesus is the Son of God, God dwelleth in him, and he in God. And we have known and believed the love that God hath to us. God is love; and he that dwelleth in love dwelleth in God, and God in him." This is the answer to the prayer Jesus prayed in John 17:26 "…that the love wherewith thou hast loved me may be in them, and I in them." He prayed the love the Father had for Him would be in us. God is love, and love is God, so he who dwells in love dwells in God and God in him.

Look at this prophetic utterance that was given during one of our meetings, as we were studying God's love:

Remove from your thinking that love is a form of nothing. Love is not a form of nothing or just a state of mind. Love is a reality. I am love.

When you are talking about love, you are not talking about a feeling. You are not talking about something that is a state. You are talking about a living being. You are talking about Me. When you speak of love, you are speaking about all that I am, all that I can do, all I ever was, and all I ever shall be *("Love—the Great Commandment" by Kenneth Copeland, the* Believer's Voice of Victory *magazine, Vol. 36, No. 3, March 2008)*

Combating the Devil

One day, the Spirit of God said to me, *You don't understand My motive when I said to turn the other cheek. If you will retaliate in My love by faith, instead of retaliating through the arm of the flesh, you can develop My power and My love in you until they are perfected, and I will keep you protected all the time.*

When Jesus said, "Turn the other cheek," He didn't intend for you to be beaten up. He intended for you to walk so powerfully in the love of God that when you do turn your other cheek, the enemy can't hit you! Look at 1 John 5:18, "...he that is begotten of God [love] keepeth himself, *and that wicked one toucheth him not.*" That is the greatest testimony of love in the physical realm. God has never asked us to be a lamb to the slaughter. Jesus was the Lamb of God. He was slaughtered in our place.

By misunderstanding God's motive in asking us to turn the other cheek, we have just laid our heads on the block and let the devil cut them off. The WORD does not say to subordinate yourself to Satan. It says, "Resist the devil, and he will flee from you" (James 4:7). But our ideas of resistance have been centered in the natural, physical realm.

We aren't in physical combat with Satan. He's a spirit being, so we must fight him with spiritual weapons. "The weapons of our warfare are not carnal, but mighty through God to the pulling down of strong holds" (2 Corinthians 10:4). These strongholds are not human. We don't wrestle with flesh and blood, but with principalities and powers, rulers of the darkness of this world and wicked spirits in heavenly places (Ephesians 6:12). Once you stop Satan's operation, you won't have any trouble with people doing you harm.

Moved by Compassion

An illustration of this is Jesus' reaction to the murder of John the Baptist. You have to remember that John and Jesus were related. In the natural realm, they were cousins, but their kinship went deeper than that. John was the only man at that time who knew Jesus was the Messiah. He was the only man who walked in the power of the Holy Spirit and in the office of prophet while Jesus was on earth, so there was a ministerial kinship between them, as well.

Then John was brutally murdered. When Jesus heard of John's death, He went to a desert place to be alone, but crowds followed Him. They made a demand on His ability. "And Jesus went forth, and saw a great multitude, and was moved with compassion toward them, and he healed their sick" (Matthew 14:14). When Jesus saw the multitude who had followed Him, He was moved with compassion—not a *feeling* of compassion, but Compassion Himself.

Compassion says, "Go ye into all the world, and preach the gospel to every creature." Compassion says, "Lay hands on the sick, and they shall recover." Compassion told Jesus to heal the sick and save the lost.

Compassion was manifest as Jesus laid hands on the sick in that desert place. Herod wasn't Jesus' enemy, Satan was. Jesus retaliated for the murder of John, not in the natural, but in the spirit. He didn't fight Herod with His fists. He reacted in the realm of the spirit, in the realm of faith and love. He retaliated against His real enemy, Satan, by healing the sick!

To understand these things, we need to understand God's motive. In commanding us to walk in love, He doesn't intend for us to be the world's whipping boys. We were not made to be spiritual rugs for Satan to wipe his feet on. God's desire is to put us in a place where we will never fail. How would you like to operate at a zero failure rate? You can, but there's only one way—through love. First Corinthians 13:8 says love *never* fails.

God's Real Motive

Let's look again at 1 John 5:18: "We know that whosoever is born of God sinneth not." This doesn't mean that if you sin you're not born of God. It means if you're born of God, you don't *practice* sin—you're not looking for a way to sin—you're doing your best to keep out of it. You could say it this way: "Whosoever is born of *love* sinneth not." So, a step out of love is a step into sin.

The second part of that verse says, "but he that is begotten of God keepeth himself, and that wicked one toucheth him not." When you're born of God, you're born of love. When you're walking the love walk, you can laugh in Satan's face. He can't harm you when you're walking in love.

God has a protective spiritual capsule that goes into effect when you get into The WORD and allow God to minister to you. God will, by His Spirit, build that capsule around you to protect you from all that's happening in the outside world. If you'll walk in The WORD, you can be protected at all times and the wicked one will not be able to touch you. That capsule is the shield of faith.

Faith works by love. Ephesians 6:16 says faith quenches *all* the fiery darts of the wicked one—not part of them, *all* of them. The first time I heard Kenneth E. Hagin say this, I was thrilled! He spoke to Satan and said, "Satan, my household is off limits to you." He put up a sign in the spirit that said, "Off limits, Satan. That means you!" Glory to God! I had always thought Satan held the key to my back door and could come and go as he pleased. Then I found out about my authority as a believer.

As you build your faith *and* begin to get an understanding of God's love down into your spirit, you will begin walking in a whole new place. Satan will have no power. You'll begin to be moved by the Spirit, by compassion, and you'll be ready to fulfill anything God has called you to do.

How do faith and love harmonize?

_____

_____

_____

Explain why love is more than just a feeling.

_____

_____

_____

Why don't you need to be afraid of the devil if you are walking in love?

_____

_____

_____

Today's
Connection Points

⊙ *Faith That Can Move Mountains* CD: "One Thing Remains (Your Love Never Fails)" (Track 6)

Feed on God's never-ending love and let it strengthen your faith as you listen to today's selection.

⊙ DVD: "The Faith and Love Connection" (Chapter 6)

Strong, overcoming faith works by love. Learn what that means and how to live the love life to receive all you need from God!

⊙ *Faith Scriptures* CD (Track 6)

1 John 4:14-16; 2 Corinthians 10:4; Ephesians 6:12; Mark 11:24-25; Galatians 5:6; 1 Corinthians 13:7-8, *The Amplified Bible;* James 2:26

Faith
in Action

Meditate on the love of God. Read what the Bible has to say about God's love.

Memorize it; get it down into your spirit. Let it become an unshakable, unstoppable reality in your life.

Notes:

_____

_____

_____

_____

_____

_____

_____

_____

_____

_____

_____

_____

_____

_____

Stay in the Flow of God's Love
by Gloria Copeland

As you've been working your way through this LifeLine Kit, we've shared with you some valuable principles of faith. You've learned that faith gives God an opening, and we've shared that faith must be spoken—all the time. Today, I want to share another core principle about faith: Faith works by love—that is—faith forgives.

Returning to Jesus' teaching on faith in Mark 11, let's read what He told His disciples right after He told them they could speak to a mountain in faith and have whatever they said.

"What things soever ye desire, when ye pray, believe that ye receive them, and ye shall have them. *And* when ye stand praying, forgive, if ye have ought against any: that your Father also which is in heaven may forgive you your trespasses" (Mark 11:24-25).

I understand that when we've been hurt and the Holy Spirit reminds us of this verse, our flesh wants to say, "Yes, but, LORD, You heard the terrible things those people said about me...." "Yes, but, LORD, You know how that person abused me...."

While the hurt we suffered may have been a cruel and ungodly act against us, nonetheless, we have to walk in love with those people. After all, God had to forgive. Jesus had to forgive. You and I are no different. We must forgive if we want to walk in faith and in the full favor of God.

Besides, if someone is against you, why do them a favor? Why let them ruin the rest of your life by short-circuiting your faith through unforgiveness?

Don't let anyone keep you sick, broke, mentally tormented and without joy because of unforgiveness. Don't help other people close the door to God's blessings in your life, and open the door to every curse loosed in this world. No, forgive them. Stay in the flow of God's love.

Faith and Love

Galatians 5:6 says, "For in Jesus Christ neither circumcision availeth any thing, nor uncircumcision; but faith which worketh by love."

Faith works by love. It is energized by love. Faith is put into motion by love. Why is that?

Well, most of us are probably familiar with the Apostle Paul's teaching on love in 1 Corinthians 13. But as we read verses 1-3 in *The Amplified Bible,* I want us to focus on the connection between faith and love.

If I [can] speak in the tongues of men and [even] of angels, but have not love...I am only a noisy gong or a clanging cymbal. And if I have prophetic powers...and if I have (sufficient) faith so that I can remove mountains, but have not love [God's love in me] I am nothing—a useless nobody. Even if I dole out all that I have [to the poor in providing] food, and if I surrender my body to be burned...but have not love...I gain nothing.

In the Garden of Eden, God gave Adam just one "do not." It was, do not eat of the tree of the knowledge of good and evil. God only gave one command, but it certainly covered a lot of territory.

Today, if you think about it, you and I still only have one "do not"—Do not get out of love. That's our one commandment. We are to walk in love, which covers a lot of ground, too. In fact, we see in this passage that our love walk is connected to everything we do in life as believers, including our faith. Paul makes it quite clear that faith—without love—is going nowhere.

Again, we have to ask ourselves: *How is it that our faith is so tied into love?* Let's read a little further into 1 Corinthians 13 and we'll find out:

> Love bears up under anything and everything that comes...its hopes are fadeless under all circumstances and it endures everything [without weakening]. Love never fails—never fades out or becomes obsolete or comes to an end... (verses 7-8, *The Amplified Bible*).

God wants us to walk in love because love never fails. He wants the best for us, and since the best is found in love, you and I must walk in love in order to receive God's best. That's why Jesus instructed His disciples to forgive when they prayed.

When you and I stand before God in prayer, in a position of faith, we must forgive anyone who has wronged us if we want answers to our prayers. Otherwise, not only do we slam the door shut on the favor of God, we also give place to what we read about in James 3:16—"For where envying and strife is, there is confusion and every evil work."

In other words, unforgiveness leads to strife, and strife to every evil work of the devil. When that happens, all the Bible reading in the world won't change the situation. Only forgiveness will.

Centered Around Love

You and I cannot pick and choose what we want to believe from God's WORD and disregard the rest. It's all connected, and it all centers around love.

What's more, as long as we're on this earth, we will have plenty of opportunities to forgive people—taking no account of evil done to us, paying no attention to suffered wrongs (1 Corinthians 13:5, *The Amplified Bible*).

Remember, faith without action is dead. "For as the body without the spirit is dead, so faith without works is dead, also" (James 2:26). If we don't act on The WORD of God and forgive, we will never walk in the full measure of God's favor. In fact, we won't even get close.

So don't take offense. Don't carry around hurts. Release them to the same blood of Jesus which cleansed you, redeemed you and set you free. Stay in the flow of God's love. As you do, you will free yourself to walk in faith...and in the full measure of God's favor!

Evening Reflection

Why is forgiveness so important?

_____

_____

_____

How does forgiveness free you?

_____

_____

_____

Who do you need to forgive today?

_____

_____

_____

Notes:

_____

_____

_____

_____

_____

_____

_____

_____

_____

_____

_____

_____

_____

_____

_____

_____

_____

Today's Prayer of Faith

Father, today, by faith in Christ Jesus, I choose to love. I choose to forgive those who have wronged me. I choose to walk fully in faith and fully in love. And, I thank You that as I do, I walk fully in Your favor and Your blessings. I thank You that, like Jesus, I too will be moved by compassion—by Your love—to minister hope, healing and truth to others. Amen!

Real-Life Testimonies
to Help Build Your Faith

Walking by Faith

Praise The LORD! A miracle has happened! My son and I received our green cards. It has been a faith walk together with our LORD for the past year. There are so many examples of how The LORD has helped me in so many areas for this green card. I was ready to give up, but then I always heard the Holy Spirit say, *Don't give up,* and a strong anointing fell over me.

During the past year I have listened to KCM teachings about faith, and they have helped me a lot. I am happy to be a Partner with you. Just to know you are there means so much to me.

A.M.H.
Sweden

Chapter Seven
Undergirding Your Faith

Faith and Patience: The Power Twins
by Kenneth Copeland

Almost everywhere you find faith mentioned in the Bible, you'll also find patience. Faith and patience are power twins. Together, they produce every time, and as you continue to work through this study on faith, I want you to understand how these two powerful forces go together.

Patience is a working power. When faith has a tendency to waver, it is patience that comes to faith's aid to make it stand. The power of patience is necessary to undergird faith. Hebrews 6:12 says, "That ye be not slothful, but followers of them who through *faith and patience* inherit the promises." And, James 1:2-4 says, "My brethren, count it all joy when ye fall into divers temptations; knowing this, that the trying of your faith worketh *patience.* But let patience have her perfect work, that ye may be perfect and entire, wanting nothing."

Patience without faith, however, has no power to call into reality the things desired. Since faith is the substance of things we hope for, patience without faith has no substance.

On the other hand, faith without patience will, many times, fail to stand firm on the written WORD that gives "title deed" to things not seen (Hebrews 11). Jesus told Peter He had prayed that Peter's faith fail not. Without the power of patience at work, sense knowledge— the things we see—can overwhelm our faith that is based on what The WORD of God says. *Patience, then, undergirds our faith and gives it endurance to persevere until the answer comes.*

Faith is a powerful force. It always works. It's not that our faith is weak and needs strength, but without the power of patience, we stop its force from working in our lives because of our negative words and actions. It's *our* faith, and we can either put it into action or stop it from working.

Traditionally, we think of patience as just "knuckling under" and being satisfied with whatever comes our way. That's not at all what patience is. It is a real force that has to be developed. Titus 2:2 says that we are to be sound, or developed, in patience.

Faith also has to be developed. The same scripture says we are to be sound in faith. Patience and faith work together the way faith and love work together. Each force plays a unique role in our Christian lives.

Common Traditions and Mistakes

It is dangerous to confuse the roles of these two forces, substituting one for the other. For instance, Hebrews 11:1 says that faith is the substance of things hoped for. Hope without faith has no substance. People say, "We are hoping and praying." This sounds good, but has no substance. In this case, hope is being confused with faith. Without the substance of faith, that kind of praying will not produce results. You can see that in a critical situation, this would be dangerous. We need to have our thinking straightened out according to the Bible, so we can use these forces properly and produce God's perfect will in our lives.

One of the most common traditions and mistakes in this area of believing is that trials and tribulations develop faith. Trials and tribulations do not develop faith. Romans 10:17 says, "Faith cometh by hearing, and hearing by The WORD of God." Trials and tribulations develop *patience*. We have already learned from James 1 that this is true. The Apostle Paul says the same thing in Romans 5:3.

Faith is developed as we act on The WORD of God. Hebrews 12:2 states that Jesus is the author and finisher, or developer, of our faith. It doesn't say Satan is the developer of our faith.

It is vitally important we realize the difference between the developing of faith and the developing of patience. Faith should be developed on The WORD of God before the trial or testing comes. Jesus says in Luke 6:47-48 that a man who acts on His words is like someone who builds his house on a rock. When the floods beat on that house, the house does not fall. Notice, the man has to dig deep. This is where his faith is developed. His *patience* is developed during the storm, but he knows his house will stand because it's built on rock. His faith is developed before the trial comes. Patience is developed in the trial or tribulation and undergirds, or keeps the door open, for faith to work.

Patience and Temptations

The definition of *patience* is "being constant" or "being the same way at all times." James 1 says we are to be single-minded. We must always respond, or react, in every circumstance of life the same way—with The WORD of God. Regardless of what may be thrown at us, we must become so WORD-of-God-minded that we don't act in fear or doubt, but always on what The WORD of our God says. The WORD says that Jesus is the same yesterday, today and forever. Jesus has always and will always respond to The WORD rather than to circumstances, reason or fear. This is the way we should be.

Being sound in patience is to answer every doubt and fear with the firm assurance and confession that God's WORD is true, no matter what we feel, hear or see. Regardless of what storms may come our way, the Father's WORD cannot fail. In that kind of atmosphere, faith is free to move and overcome whatever Satan has put in our way.

To properly develop the power of patience, we must know what the Bible says about testings and trials. Take a moment to open your Bible and read James 1:12-21. The Greek word translated *temptations* in these scriptures is the same word for "trials" and "testings." It is vitally important that we know, from verse 13, that God is not tested by evil, and He doesn't tempt or test men with evil. We are warned never to say that we are tested by God.

Verse 14 explains what a test or trial is. It's anything that applies pressure on the lusts or desires of the flesh. *Any pressure that draws us away from God's WORD is the beginning of a test.* If we then act on that lust, sin is the result. Still, we have a way of escape, because The WORD says we have an advocate with the Father—Jesus Christ. He is faithful to forgive us our sins when we confess them (1 John 1:9). When Satan applies pressure on our bodies to make them sick, we don't have to succumb to that pressure. When he presents us with financial ruin, we don't have to yield to the temptation to turn to the world and borrow. Most of the time, this only makes matters worse. Thank God, we can turn to God's WORD in Philippians 4:19 and use our faith. Then, regardless of circumstances, we exercise the power of patience and continue to stand fast in the liberty to which we have been called (Galatians 5:1).

First Corinthians 10:13 says, "There hath no temptation taken you but such as is common to man: but God is faithful, who will not suffer you to be tempted above that ye are able; but will with the temptation also make a way to escape, that ye may be able to bear it." This scripture reveals three more important things about trials:

1. Testings and temptations are common to man. No one is ever tested or tried with things that are not common to mankind. Satan does not have the right to call upon his experience as a heavenly being to apply things that are outside the realm of humanity as tests or trials.

2. God is faithful. You will never face anything you cannot overcome.

3. God always provides the way of escape.

Satan's weapons are no match for the weapons God has provided for us. Thank God, the weapons of our warfare are not carnal but powerful *through God* to the pulling down of strongholds. Satan is limited to the things that are common to mankind, but we are not. We have access to the full armor of God Himself. Our patience rests solidly on the full assurance that, no matter what comes next, Jesus has provided more than enough victory to put us over.

No matter what trial you are facing—sickness, financial ruin, broken relationships and whatever the devil can throw at you—you must exercise your faith in God's WORD. Then, let patience have its perfect work. The force of faith will be at work, undergirded by the power of patience. Your faith will connect with the Father the very moment you take His WORD as the evidence of your breakthrough. Now, confess with your mouth that what you are believing for is yours, and by your actions show that it's yours. Patience will begin to work from the moment you believe you receive, and it will be allowed to work until the victory is completely yours. The voice of patience says, "I know God's WORD is true. I will not be moved by what I see or feel. I will only be moved by The WORD of God. I patiently rest on the truth of God's mighty WORD!"

How are faith and patience developed?

_____

_____

_____

What is the definition of patience? How does this definition differ from your past understanding of it?

_____

_____

_____

What three things can you learn about temptation from 1 Corinthians 10:13? Does this change the way you perceive the temptations you now face? If so, how?

_____

_____

_____

Today's
Connection Points

- **_Faith That Can Move Mountains_ CD: "The Anthem/ Hallelujah" (Track 7)**

    As you let patience have its perfect work in your situation, keep praising God for providing your answer!

- **DVD: "Faith and Patience" (Chapter 7)**

    These two powerful forces work hand in hand to bring us through to victory. Learn how to harness these power twins to triumph in every situation.

- **_Faith Scriptures_ CD (Track 7)**

    Hebrews 6:12; James 1:2-4; Titus 2:2; Hebrews 12:2; Luke 6:47-48; Galatians 5:1; 1 Corinthians 10:13; Luke 12:32

Faith
in Action

Begin seeing your temptation, or trial, through The WORD of God.

Let your faith and patience work together until your breakthrough is complete and you have the full manifestation of your victory.

Notes:

_____

_____

_____

_____

_____

_____

_____

Developing Patience
by Gloria Copeland

When Ken and I first began to walk by faith, we were in a terrible financial condition. It would have been very easy at the time to give up and quit. But as the laws of prosperity became reality to us, the light at the end of the tunnel became brighter and brighter. Still, our debts were not taken care of immediately. It took some time for us to pay all our bills. During this period, we put the force of patience to work and refused to give up. In less than one year, we were free from debt and headed on a path to victory.

You may be facing a similar financial situation, like we were. Or, you may be facing an illness or some other devastating circumstance. That's why it's so good that you are working through this Faith LifeLine Kit. As Ken and I have shared in the last several days, faith is the key to overcoming any challenge in life. It's a powerful force in the Christian life, but right alongside it, and working with it, is patience.

What exactly does patience have to do with faith? Patience undergirds and sustains faith until the result is manifest. When you learn to release the power of patience, you can receive anything from God that agrees with His WORD. This is where most people have failed when attempting to walk by faith. But it doesn't have to be so. Patience is the difference between trying and doing. Some people go fishing and others catch fish. Some attempt to walk by faith; others succeed. Patience makes the difference.

When Trouble Comes

In the face of adversity when it looks like doom is inevitable, Satan puts strong pressure on you to faint and give up. At that moment, you want to succumb to the pressure and let go of God's WORD. Don't do it! You cannot succumb to Satan's pressure without flinging away your confidence in God's WORD. To act on Satan's pressure, you have to lay down the promises found in the Bible. There is no middle ground. When it comes to standing on The WORD, you are either on or off.

Patience has the courage to refuse what Satan tries to prove true in the natural world: "I will not succumb to pressure. I am moved by nothing except The WORD of God."

When Satan's pressure says that God's WORD is not working, patience rejects it as a lie. Patience has no fear. Patience knows that God's WORD has never failed. Patience knows that when faith is exercised to receive God's WORD, success is inevitable.

If you are to please God, you must operate in faith. Faith not only believes that God exists but that God rewards those who diligently seek Him. Why is it that God takes no pleasure in you if you draw back in fear? Because the instant you draw back in fear, you quit operating in faith. "Fear not, little flock; for it is your Father's good pleasure to give you the kingdom" (Luke 12:32).

We are believers, not doubters. Faith, undergirded by the power of patience, defends and protects the soul from Satan's attack. Faith is the assurance of the things we believe we have received. Faith in God's WORD is our proof that we have received, even though we cannot yet see it with our natural eye. That kind of faith comes only through God's grace and the power of patience. Remain steadfast, regardless of what situation you are facing. Don't give up, but continue to put The WORD first place in every situation.

Evening Reflection

How do faith and patience work together?

_____

_____

_____

_____

How does patience work when pressure from the enemy challenges God's promises?

_____

_____

_____

_____

In what situations can you proactively exercise your patience this coming week?

_____

_____

_____

_____

Notes:

_____

_____

_____

_____

_____

_____

_____

_____

_____

Today's
Prayer of Faith

Father God, I choose to exercise patience, today. I will let it undergird my faith and keep my focus on Your promises. When I face tests and trials, I will stand on Your WORD without wavering. And I know You will give me Your grace and strength to see it through! In Jesus' Name. Amen.

Real-Life Testimonies
to Help Build Your Faith

Supercharged Faith Stills the Storm

After my son and I left the Southwest Believers' Convention, we came home to find a hurricane fast approaching, but our faith was supercharged and ready to rebuke the winds! We live in Port Charlotte, Florida, which was almost at the center of the storm and only one or two miles from the water.

We had no phone, water or power for a time, but other than that we suffered very little loss due to the storm. My home is surrounded by oak trees, and many fell around us but none touched my condo. My son and I were unscathed! We were able to stay with friends until power was restored, and since my work is done via the Internet, I only lost minimal wages. I just have to brag on our LORD!

Rose Marie
Florida

Chapter Eight
Stretch Your Faith

Stretch Your Faith
by Kenneth Copeland

There's never been a greater time to stretch our faith. Right now, in these end times, we have a greater opportunity to live victoriously on this earth than any other generation since Jesus was resurrected and seated at the right hand of glory.

As you're using this LifeLine Kit and building your faith with The WORD, begin to put a demand on it. Exercise it regularly to enlarge its capacity to overcome every challenge and receive bigger and greater things from The WORD of God. You should do this on a regular basis.

Remember, it's God's own faith that dwells in you, and Jesus is the developer of it. It will grow if you feed and exercise it.

Too often we've been quick to settle for "good enough" instead of God's best. We do that with our calling, our health, our relationships—and that's especially true where our finances are concerned.

The devil would like nothing better than to keep us bound by debt, lack, poverty and financial weakness in order to keep us under the thumb of the world's ungodly way of doing things. He'd like nothing better than to render us impotent and without influence in worldly affairs. Not to mention cutting us short and preventing us from getting God's WORD out to the sick and dying masses of people who need Jesus so badly!

Here we are, the generation that has been given more equipment both in technology and spiritual revelation with which to reach mankind than any other generation, and we've been so bogged down in debt and lack, we haven't been doing what we should have.

Think about this: Even in our bound and bogged-down condition, the Body of Christ has still affected the whole world with the gospel of Jesus. Think about what is about to happen as more and more of God's people are set free to give and go—by the millions. Wow!

Stretching and Pushing

Now, let me share with you what I mean by stretching and putting a demand on your faith, because this is an important principle as you're learning about faith in this LifeLine Kit. Look at your own situation and surroundings, and decide what the next step up should be. Where *should* you be in your giving? Where *should* you be in your income? How *should* your physical body feel? Where *should* you be in the call God has put on your life? What's the next step toward *what should be?*

Now, go to The WORD and believe Philippians 4:13—you can do all things through God's Anointed One and His Anointing which strengthens you. Begin to think of yourself that way: free in Jesus, doing God's best instead of being satisfied, or worse yet, just putting up with things the way they are.

Believe me, things will either get better by faith and grow or they'll get worse. They won't just stay the same.

Sometimes, the very mention of living debt-free sets off a storm of unbelief. I was praying about this recently, and The LORD said, *When people ask, "Brother Copeland, how could we ever build a new church without borrowing money? It's so much," tell them, "If you don't have the faith to build the church without going into debt, you won't have the faith to make the payments."*

It takes the same faith to believe God for cash up front as it does to believe Him for 30 or 40 years of big payments, and all that interest that's going into the world's pockets. The same would be true of a home or any other project that's dedicated to God and to your welfare.

Now, that's what I mean by stretching your faith. Don't build a church or a house or whatever it is, before you spend enough time meditating on God's WORD to know in your heart you really can do all things through Jesus and His Anointing which strengthens you. During that meditation and faith-stretching time in The WORD, you will hear from God. He'll show you what to do. He'll show you how to do it. He'll show you when to do it. And, He'll finance you.

You belong to Him. It gives Him great pleasure to prosper you, especially when you go to Him instead of the world to get your needs met. This goes for your health, relationships, calling and all other areas of your life, too.

The WORD Is Key

As always and in everything, The WORD of God is the key. It must come first. The bigger the problem or project, the more The WORD of God should be your first priority and should get all your attention—not the other way around.

Don't give your attention to the size of the challenge. Give your attention to The WORD. Whatever you are believing God for—no matter how big or problematic—will begin to lose its formidability. It will begin to shrink, and you'll laugh and say, "My God meets my needs according to *His* riches in glory." That's when you're ready to go ahead with the project and win.

Gloria and I have lived this way since 1967, and I can tell you The WORD works! Put it to work. Push yourself to start stretching your faith today.

Morning Reflection

In what areas have you settled for "good enough" instead of God's best?

_____

_____

_____

_____

_____

Examine your calling, your relationships, finances and health. Where should each of them be today?

_____

_____

_____

What should get your attention when faced with a problem or concern?

_____

_____

_____

Today's
Connection Points

- *Faith That Can Move Mountains* **CD: "No Chains on Me" (Track 8)**

  As you listen to today's selection, get in agreement with God's WORD and let your faith grow beyond your circumstances.

- **DVD: "Wake Up Your Faith" (Chapter 8)**

  Learn how words spoken in faith can change your life. Rise up, break out of the circumstances that hold you down, and receive your breakthrough!

- *Faith Scriptures* **CD (Track 8)**

  Proverbs 28:20; Romans 4:18-21; Romans 5:1-2, *The Amplified Bible;* Galatians 3:13-14; 1 Corinthians 1:9; Colossians 2:2-3; Mark 9:23

Faith
in Action

Stretch your faith and make a quality decision to be faithful in your walk with The LORD, today.
As you are full of faith, your blessings will abound!

Notes:

_____

_____

_____

Faithfulness: Being Full of Faith
by Gloria Copeland

When it comes to living a life of faith, there's a fruit of the spirit you need to develop: faithfulness. Sometimes people say to me, "I'm having trouble walking consistently in faith. I'm strong in The LORD one day and weak the next."

If that's how you feel, no problem! Faithfulness is a fruit of the spirit that flourishes when you maintain a living connection with God. So if you're lacking in faithfulness, all you need to do is start spending time each day fellowshiping with The LORD in His WORD.

The dictionary defines *faithfulness* as being "(1) full of faith; believing; strong or firm in one's faith, (2) firmly adhering to duty; of true fidelity, loyal, true to allegiance; constant in the performances of duties or services." To be faithful is to be trustworthy and dependable. If you want a perfect picture of faithfulness, look at God Himself, for He is faithful (1 Corinthians 1:9)!

Actually, the Greek word for *faithfulness* used in the New Testament can also be translated *faith*. So faith and faithfulness are very closely related.

You might say it this way: Faith is faithfulness to God's WORD. Faith is being faithful to believe what God says, even when circumstances, obstacles or people seem to contradict His WORD.

Daily time in The WORD and fellowship with The LORD causes you to grow in faithfulness. It strengthens you in your walk of faith so that you can reach out and receive the blessings of God, blessings like healing, prosperity and protection. Proverbs 28:20 promises, "A faithful man shall abound with blessings."

You see, Jesus has already bought everything we need in this life with His blood. As Galatians 3:13-14 says:

> Christ hath redeemed us from the curse of the law, being made a curse for us: for it is written, Cursed is every one that hangeth on a tree: that the blessing of Abraham might come on the Gentiles through Jesus Christ; that we might receive the promise of the Spirit through faith.

If you'll read Deuteronomy 28, you'll see that every good thing imaginable is included in God's blessing, and every bad thing imaginable is included in the curse. So we're set up in style! God has already provided everything we could ever need. We don't have to talk Him into giving us these things. They're already ours. The blessing has "come upon us"!

All we have to do is put ourselves in a position to receive. And, the primary key to receiving is *faithfulness*. We must be faithful to believe and faithful to act on The WORD of God.

Of course, before you can even begin to believe God's WORD, you must know what He has said. You must do more than casually read it now and then. You must believe it and act on it consistently. And to do that, you must have confidence in the One who spoke that WORD. You must have confidence in God.

Such confidence is developed by spending time with Him. Just as you grow to trust another person (assuming he is a trustworthy person) by getting to know him better, by listening to him speak and deepening your relationship with him, so it is with God. The more time you spend with Him, the better you will know Him—and the better you know Him, the greater will be your confidence in Him.

That confidence will enable you to faithfully take God at His WORD. You won't sit around wondering if He will do what He said. You won't believe Him one day and doubt Him the next. You'll be able to believe and act consistently as if His WORD is true even when circumstances try to tell you it isn't.

When you're in The WORD and fellowshiping with God every day, you'll be able to look beyond the circumstances staring you in the face and screaming at you, *"You'll go bankrupt!"* or, *"You'll die young!"* You'll have the strength of character to see past those circumstances and focus, instead, on the power and love of God and His ability to bring you through in victory.

In his book on the fruit of the spirit, Donald Gee wonderfully illustrates how living fellowship with the Spirit of God brings forth faithfulness in our lives. "Our human natures in all their unreliability [are like]...the loose powder of cement," he says. "But, when water is mixed with the cement it turns into concrete hard as a rock. So the living water of God's Holy Spirit can turn our lack of steadfastness into magnificent faithfulness, and convert many an impulsive 'Simon' into a devoted 'Peter.'"[1]

That, in itself, is reason enough to spend time every day in The WORD and in prayer. But there are more reasons still!

Staying in living contact with God will not only cause faithfulness to flourish; it will cause all the rest of the fruit of the spirit to grow in your life, too. It will empower you to walk in love, and that's vital because love never fails!

Staying in living contact with God will enable you to live in peace and be full of joy. It will also strengthen your ability to be patient. As we recently learned, patience is a powerful force that undergirds your faith and keeps you from quitting when tests and trials come. When patience is operating in your life, instead of succumbing to the pressure of circumstances, you can keep on believing God.

So, get in The WORD consistently, every day, and develop the fruit of faithfulness in your life. When you do, you'll find living by faith is the only way to live!

---

1 (Donald Gee, *The Fruit of the Spirit* [Springfield: Gospel Publishing House, 1928], p. 60, used by permission of the publisher.)

Define faithfulness.

_____

_____

_____

_____

_____

How are faithfulness and faith related?

_____

_____

_____

_____

How do patience and faithfulness work together? How does this combination affect your faith?

_____

_____

_____

_____

Notes:

_____

_____

_____

_____

_____

_____

_____

_____

_____

_____

_____

_____

_____

_____

_____

Today's
Prayer of Faith

Father God, as I'm faithful, I know You will cause me to abound with blessings! Help me to be consistent as I make a quality decision to seek after You with my whole heart, every day—no matter what challenges I face. You are my LORD, and I am stretching my faith to overcome every challenge that comes my way. In Jesus' Name. Amen.

Real-Life Testimonies
to Help Build Your Faith

Everything Is Going to Be All Right

Eighteen years ago my husband and I were married. He was a nonbeliever and my faith walk was small. Today, he's attending church, praising God, believing with me and turning to God about our circumstances.

His favorite thing to say is "pray about it." I stood fast declaring him to be a man of radical integrity with a heart after Jesus. Through your ministry I've grown leaps and bounds, and he's hooked on Jesus as much as I am. Everything is going to be all right, and Jesus is LORD!

C.L.F.
Canada

Chapter Nine
Fearless Faith

Faith or Fear: The Choice Is Yours

by Kenneth Copeland

So far, we've seen how God cannot do anything for you apart or separate from faith. That's a spiritual principle. But, did you know there's another spiritual principle in action, too? It's this: Satan cannot do anything to you apart or separate from *fear*.

Fear is Satan's source of power the way faith is God's source of power. Satan has people operating in fear, and they don't even know it. This is very important to understand when learning about how faith works, because fear and faith don't mix.

Like many believers, you might find yourself running into a problem because instead of being overtaken by the blessings of God, some portion of the curse is clinging to you. It might be sickness or lack, failure in relationships or business dealings. But whatever it is, it is clearly of the devil and it is sticking to you like gum to your shoe.

Hopefully, by this point in this LifeLine Kit, you realize that God is not your problem. He is on your side. And, neither He nor His WORD *ever* fails.

You might be tempted to believe the devil is your problem. But, the fact is, you know better than that, too. Jesus whipped him completely 2,000 years ago and took away all his authority.

The question is: If God isn't the problem, and the devil isn't the problem...who is?

If you've found yourself wondering that lately, don't feel bad. Every believer who has ever gone through a study like this has asked that question. At one time or another we've all found ourselves unable to succeed for reasons we don't understand.

A Lesson in Reciprocals

Why is that?

For the most part, we haven't grasped the basic spiritual operating principles of this planet. We've learned a little about the force of faith and the principles of God. But there's more going on here. A lot more.

You see, for every force and principle God has created, there exists a reciprocal.

When God first told me that, I had to get out my dictionary and look up *reciprocal* to find out exactly what that meant. I found it referred to something which corresponds to something else, but is reversed or inverted. The reciprocal of north, for example, is south. North and south are both directions on the compass. The difference is, one is the opposite of the other. No matter how far you go north, the moment you turn around, you will be going south because they are reciprocals.

If you were the navigator of a ship, you'd be at a great disadvantage if you didn't know south existed, wouldn't you? If the only direction you were aware of was north, you'd get off track very easily.

That sounds silly but the truth is, many Christians are trying to do that very thing in the realm of the spirit. They are trying to navigate by faith without taking into consideration the reciprocal force that can, and will, take them in the opposite direction if they don't guard against it.

What is this reciprocal force I'm talking about? It's the force of fear.

"Oh, I don't feel like I'm afraid of anything," you may say.

That doesn't really matter because fear is not a feeling. It is not an emotion. It is a spiritual force. And, although it can and does affect your emotions, it can be in operation even when you don't feel it.

To understand just how powerful fear can be, you must first realize the devil didn't create it. He can't create anything. He is not a creator. He is just a fallen angel, and the Bible says, "There is no truth in him" (John 8:44).

If he had ever originated anything, it would be a truth. But he hasn't. All he can do is take what God has created and pervert it. So that's exactly what he does. He takes the powerful principles God put in force to bless mankind and twists them so they work in reverse and bring a curse instead.

Faith Reversed Becomes a Curse

That's what happened in the Garden of Eden. Before the devil got involved, Adam and Eve were living in total blessing. They were ruling with the authority God had given them over a planet that was governed by one master law—the law of the Spirit of life. Heaven and earth were spiritually connected by The WORD of God so everything good that comes from that divine life flowed freely without obstruction.

What happened?

You know the story. The devil came and questioned The WORD of God. He said to Eve, "Yea, hath God said...?" Then, once he had her attention, he flatly contradicted God's WORD. "Ye shall not surely die," he said (see Genesis 3:2-4).

He deceived Eve into breaking fellowship with God and His WORD through disobedience. Adam followed suit, though he knew better. By the time he was done, the devil had gained dominion over mankind, and therefore over the earth God had given them to rule. He had taken the master law of the Spirit of life and perverted it into its reciprocal: the law of sin and death.

Under the law of sin and death, every blessing became a curse. The ground which had once produced abundantly began to withhold its fruit, and prosperity became poverty. Health was turned to sickness. Success became failure. Victory turned to defeat.

What's more, faith, the creative power of God He had given to man to use to rule the earth, became fear. So, when God came walking in the Garden of Eden in the cool of the day to fellowship with man, "Adam and his wife hid themselves from the presence of The LORD God amongst the trees of the garden. And The LORD God called unto Adam, and said unto him, Where art thou? And he said, I heard thy voice in the garden, and I was afraid..." (Genesis 3:8-10).

Two Master Laws

But, thankfully, that's not the end of the story. God didn't abandon the earth and leave man forever enslaved to the devil and the law of sin and death. He sent His own Son in the form of man to reverse what Adam had done. He sent Jesus, not only to the cross, but into hell itself to pay the price for sin and bear its penalty. Then, by raising Jesus from the dead, God reinstated the law of the Spirit of life for whosoever would believe on Him.

Romans 8:1-2 says it this way: "There is therefore now no condemnation to them which are in Christ Jesus, who walk not after the flesh, but after the Spirit. For the law of the Spirit of life in Christ Jesus hath made me free from the law of sin and death."

That means there are now two master laws functioning in the earth: God's original, the law of the Spirit of life—and Satan's reciprocal, or counterfeit—which is the law of sin and death. As far as God is concerned, every believer has been delivered from Satan's law and all its effects. Jesus has done everything necessary to set us free.

Yet, in spite of that fact, vestiges of the curse often seem to dog the steps of many Christians because they unknowingly activate the law of sin and death and give the devil entrance into their lives. As Hosea 4:6 says, they are "destroyed for lack of knowledge."

Look at the chart below, and you will see exactly what I'm talking about. I have listed the two master laws along with their authors and some of the results they produce. You'll notice each part corresponds with its reciprocal. It's the same—yet opposite.

The law of the Spirit of life	The law of sin and death
Jesus Christ	*Satan*
the new birth	spiritual death
the Baptism in the Holy Spirit	demonic oppression
righteousness	unrighteousness
healing	sickness
prosperity	poverty
love	hate
success	failure

Study the left-hand side of that list for a moment, then see if you can answer this question: What is the force that activates the law of the Spirit of life?

It's faith! We receive the new birth by faith. We receive the Baptism in the Holy Spirit by faith. We receive healing by faith. Nothing happens in the realm of *life*—God's realm—without faith.

Now, apply the law of reciprocals, and you'll see that since fear is the satanic reciprocal of faith, the law of sin and death is activated by fear! Not just occasionally—but *every* time.

Repent and Get Rid of It

"Well, I wasn't afraid and I still went bankrupt, and the devil stole everything I had."

That's impossible. The devil cannot prevail in your life apart from fear any more than God can prevail in your life apart from faith.

Just as "faith is the substance of things hoped for" (Hebrews 11:1), fear is the substance of things not desired. Faith reaches into the unseen realm of the spirit and manifests the promises of God. Fear reaches into the unseen realm and manifests the threats of the devil. Faith is the power God uses to create. Fear is the power the devil uses to destroy.

Hebrews 2:14-15 says Jesus became flesh and blood "...that through death he might destroy him that had the power of death, that is, the devil; and deliver them who through fear of death were all their lifetime subject to bondage." It's fear of death that keeps us in bondage.

You must understand, however, that fear of death does not necessarily mean you're afraid to leave your body and head for heaven, as believers do when they die physically. (You're probably looking forward to that day!) The fear of death referred to in Hebrews has a much broader meaning than that. It includes the fear of sickness, lack, failure and everything else that is included under the master law of sin and death.

But, we don't have to live in fear. God said, "Fear not!" more than 60 times in the Bible. He wouldn't have given us that command if we didn't have the power to obey it.

In Psalm 118:6, David said, "The LORD is on my side; I will not fear...." Notice he didn't say, "I'll pray and ask God to take the fear away." He didn't say, "I will try not to be afraid." He said, "I WILL NOT FEAR."

The Real Overcomes the Phony Every Time

You might as well face it. As long as you are on this earth, the devil is going to talk to you. He has a right to test your faith by bringing you circumstances and lies to see if you'll receive them.

But, when he does, refuse them. Cast down those fearful imaginations and every thought that is contrary to the promise of God (2 Corinthians 10:5). Like David, say, "The LORD is on my side, I WILL NOT FEAR!"

Then, open your mouth and speak The WORD of God. Use it to contradict the devil's lies. If he tells you that you won't have enough money to pay your house payment this month, don't just struggle silently with that thought. Speak up. Say right out loud, "I *will* have the money to pay my house payment. I know I will because my God supplies all my needs according to His riches in glory by Christ Jesus!"

I found out a long time ago that when my mouth speaks, my mind has to stop and listen to what it's saying. Maybe you won't fully believe that confession the first time you make it. But if you'll keep saying it, you'll keep hearing it. And, eventually, your faith will be so strong and your heart so full, you'll start speaking with total confidence.

That's when the devil will run for cover because fear has no chance when faith comes on the scene. Faith is the original. Fear is the counterfeit. And, the real overcomes the phony every time!

Morning Reflection

How is fear the reciprocal of faith?

_____
_____
_____
_____

What are the two master laws in motion on this earth? How do they differ?

_____
_____
_____
_____
_____

What does it take to refuse to fear? How can you apply this to your situation?

_____
_____
_____
_____
_____

Today's Connection Points

⦿ *Faith That Can Move Mountains* **CD: "Never Once" (Track 9)**

Don't give doubt or fear any room in your thinking! Feed on God's faithfulness and let it become bigger than the problem.

⦿ **DVD: "Fear Versus Faith" (Chapter 9)**

Learn the importance of reciprocals and what they mean to your faith. Don't let a lack of knowledge defeat *your* faith!

⦿ *Faith Scriptures* **CD (Track 9)**

Romans 8:1-2; Hebrews 2:14-15; Psalm 118:6; 2 Corinthians 13:5, *The Amplified Bible;* Hebrews 10:35-36, *The Amplified Bible;* Hebrews 10:38-39, *The Amplified Bible;* Habakkuk 2:4, *New Living Translation;* Hebrews 10:23

Faith in Action

Refuse to operate in fear today.

Whenever you feel a negative emotion or a negative thought rise up, contradict it with the truth of God's WORD.

Notes:

_____

_____

_____

_____

_____

_____

_____

_____

_____

_____

_____

_____

_____

_____

_____

_____

_____

_____

_____

_____

_____

_____

_____

_____

_____

_____

_____

_____

_____

_____

_____

_____

_____

You Can Have Fearless Faith

by Gloria Copeland

Ken and I have walked by faith for a long time, but we regularly go back and refresh ourselves on the principles of faith so we don't let things slip. I hope after you've finished this LifeLine Kit, you don't just put it on the shelf. If you really want to be a spiritual powerhouse with "fearless faith," you need to review the principles you're learning here on a regular basis. Ken and I do that all the time. We make certain we're not missing some of the elements that bring the power of God into our lives. *The Amplified Bible* says it this way: "Examine and test and evaluate your own selves to see whether you are holding to your faith and showing the proper fruits of it. Test and prove yourselves…" (2 Corinthians 13:5).

How do we keep ourselves walking with "fearless faith" every day? We simply have to continue to keep His WORD in front of our eyes and in our ears. What you hear and see gets down into your heart. Whether good things or bad things, what you focus on becomes what you believe. Focus on what The WORD says, and you will have victory in every situation.

You are the one in control of what goes into your eyes and ears. You are responsible for what gets into your heart—for what you believe. Put your eyes and ears on The WORD of God. Receive it and believe it. As we've learned throughout this study, this is how faith comes.

Agree With The WORD and Don't Quit!

When you say from your heart what God says about anything in your life, you can be sure the thing you're believing for will manifest. Just don't quit!

Hebrews 10:35 tells us, "Do not, therefore, fling away your fearless confidence, for it carries a great and glorious compensation of reward" *(The Amplified Bible).*

I like to call it "fearless faith" because fearless confidence in God's WORD *is* faith.

When you get so full of The WORD that it becomes bigger in you than the situation, when you are not moved by what you see or what you hear, you've moved into a place of fearless faith.

How do you develop fearless faith? Well, you grow up into it.

Ken and I grew up in our faith, and today it's easy for us to walk by faith when needs arise or challenges come. We have no doubt or fear even when the answer to our challenge seems to be delayed. We know it's coming. In the early days, I knew that from the Bible, but today I also know it from experience. Faith in God's WORD always produces results!

The WORD you continue to place in your heart through your eyes and ears—The WORD that you speak in agreement with God—will increase your faith. You may have been the world's worst worrier. You may have been someone who believed things wouldn't change unless you changed them yourself. Or you may have even been someone whose tendency had always been to throw in the towel and give up.

Don't fall back into your old ways. Keep on The WORD. Replace worrying with believing. Agree with The WORD of God, and don't give up. Stand fast and be patient. Eventually, you will receive what God has promised. You will inherit the promise!

Faith keeps us moving in the direction and on the path God has planned for our lives. We hear, we believe, we speak, we receive—we get there!

Keep Company With Strong Believers

One of the ways to develop your faith is to watch the company you keep. You have to make sure you don't surround yourself with people who think and speak negatively. Remember what Ken taught this morning. Fear is the opposite of faith, and the world will preach the law of sin and death to you all the time.

The smartest thing you can do is to keep company with people who are more turned on and tuned in to God than you are. Those are the kind of people who will help you develop your faith. Choose friends who believe God and know how to stand fast—even in the hardest of times. If you want to develop fearless faith, seek out people who are full of faith and led by the Spirit—then stick with them! You have to help each other. Once you have developed strong faith yourself, you will be in a place to help other people who are growing. But always be connected to someone who has stronger faith than yours.

You can grow by yourself if you have to, but when The LORD brings people into your life to help you grow, hang on to them and learn all you can about the fearless faith you see in them.

Preserve Your Soul

Hebrews 10:39 says: "We are of those who believe [who cleave to and trust in and rely on God through Jesus Christ, the Messiah] and by faith preserve the soul" *(The Amplified Bible)*.

Do you see that? We believe and preserve our souls *by faith!*

What is your soul? It is your mind, will and emotions…what you think, how you make decisions and how you express yourself. Your faith in God's WORD changes your soul to agree with Him. Your way of thinking, making decisions and expressing yourself begins to line up with The WORD of God. Your changed soul is where "walking by faith" is played out. Your soul should come into agreement with your reborn spirit and allow God to direct your steps every day.

Before Ken and I were born again, we weren't even thinking about God, or how He would do things. We didn't know, and we didn't care. Now that we're believers, things are different. We have His WORD in our hearts and we're growing in faith. Our souls have been changed, and everything we do now, we should do in line with The WORD.

We know things change by faith. And much of it has to do with your soul changing and being obedient to The WORD of God. You change and things change!

It Starts With a Choice

Habakkuk 2:4 says, "The righteous will live by their faith" *(New Living Translation)*. There are actually two meanings we can get from that verse. For one, it means *the way you live* or *your manner of life*. In other words, your way of living is faith thinking, faith talking, faith acting. It also means your *means of life*—your very life and well-being is by faith.

To live by faith, you have to give God His place in your life. He's not going to barge into your life and take over. He doesn't operate like the devil does. The devil is a liar and a thief. He comes into your life uninvited to steal all he can from you and to kill. He will do everything he can to keep you from the life of faith.

The choice is yours. Jesus said, "I am come that they might have life, and that they might have it more abundantly" (John 10:10). John tells us Jesus came to destroy the works of the devil (1 John 3:8). If you don't choose Jesus and go the direction God has for you, you're choosing to walk right into the plan of the devil to destroy your life.

The starting place for your life of faith is to say, "Come into my life, LORD Jesus. I accept You as my Savior. I want You to lead and direct my life. Take my life and do something with it."

Receive Him and all that He has in store for you.

Never Let Go

As Christians, we should believe what God says more than what we see with our eyes or what the world or the devil says to us. We refuse to be moved off our faith.

Paul declared in Hebrews 10:23, "Let us hold fast the profession of our faith without wavering; (for he is faithful that promised)." The key is to never let go, never give up and never stop growing in faith. You keep faith growing by staying in The WORD of God. Keep faith alive in your heart by relying on God to be true to His WORD.

Lay hold of faith, and don't let go! Nothing on this earth can take your faith, and you certainly are not going to give it up. If you hold fast to your fearless faith, you will receive the reward—because *He is faithful who promised!*

You are born again to live a life of bold, fearless and unwavering faith.

Evening Reflection

What does it mean to have "fearless faith"?

_____

_____

_____

_____

What are some changes you can make in your life today to help you walk in fearless faith every day?

_____

_____

_____

_____

What are the two meanings behind Habakkuk 2:4, which states, "The righteous will live by their faith"?

_____

_____

_____

_____

_____

Notes:

Today's Prayer of Faith

*LORD God, today I want to live a life that is ruled and operated by faith!
Give me wisdom to see when fear tries to nudge its way in, and remind
me to open my mouth and boldly speak out Your promises, instead. I
will fill my heart with Your WORD and live fearlessly by faith! In Jesus'
Name. Amen.*

Real-Life Testimonies
to Help Build Your Faith

No More Cravings

Not long ago, Kenneth Copeland talked on the broadcast about God setting him free
from overeating and the desire for sugar. That inspired faith in me, and I asked God to set
me free. The scripture He gave me was, "If the Son therefore shall make you free, ye shall
be free indeed" (John 8:36).

I started confessing every day: "Thank You, LORD, that I am free from greed and gluttony,
free from overeating and comfort eating and free from the desire for sugars, fat or
chocolate."

Until I started doing this, I used to crave chocolate and would eat some most days. I
continued to confess the scripture, and for a while, I was still eating chocolate and sweet
things. After a holiday abroad where I didn't eat any chocolate, I came home and to my
delight, I found that not only did I not desire it, but I actually *disliked* it!

Since then, the same thing has happened regarding cakes, biscuits, coffee and other
sweet things. Like Kenneth said, I don't have to resist, I just don't like them anymore. The
side effect is that I have lost more than 21 pounds! Others have noticed my weight loss,
and I have been able to give my testimony—and give the glory to God!

**S.B.
England**

Chapter Ten
Living by Faith

Faith—The Key to Unlimited Treasure!
by Kenneth Copeland

In this LifeLine Kit, we've been talking a lot about faith, and Gloria and I could go on and on. Every time we arrive at a place where we think we know a little bit about faith, the Holy Spirit opens a whole new insight into the wonders of faith in God!

As we close this study, I want to leave you with a final thought in these last two teaching articles: *Faith is the doorway to abundance.* It's the key to unlimited treasure. Its laws of operations are sure, steadfast and as unchanging as Jesus Himself, and apply to every area of life—spiritual, mental, physical, financial, relational and professional. Faith should cover every area of your life. In giving Himself to us, Jesus has given us His faith—not just a portion of it, all of it. He did not give us only a portion of Himself. Everything He has and is has been given to us in full measure.

Colossians 2:3 says all the treasures of wisdom and knowledge are hidden in Him. Well, that's where we are—in Him. Verses 9-10 of that same chapter are shoutin' ground: "For in him dwelleth all the fulness of the Godhead bodily. And ye are complete in him, which is the head of all principality and power."

You have the same right to use the faith of God as Jesus does. After all, He's as much your Father as He is Jesus' Father. You're as much His child as Jesus is. Does the scripture only say all things are possible with God? No, it also says all things are possible *to the believer.*

It is up to you and me just how far we go with the faith He has given us. The only limits placed on the growth of our faith are there because of us, not because the Father has limited it in any way. The growth of our faith is in direct proportion to the time spent developing it. It's not like the growth of natural things that have built-in limitations. Faith will continue to grow until it becomes however large it has to be to overcome whatever the storms of life bring against us.

Satan is limited. Everything, thank God, in this world of sin and death is defeated. Faith is unlimited. Why? Because its source is unlimited.

Faith is born out of The WORD Himself: "Faith cometh by hearing, and hearing by The WORD of God" (Romans 10:17). And that's how we are born again. We are born again "not of corruptible seed, but of incorruptible, by The WORD of God, which liveth and abideth for ever" (1 Peter 1:23). That's why faith is so easy for the person who spends time in The WORD. It's as natural to the life of the believer as swimming is to a fish. It's what we were born to do—BELIEVE!

The Growth Process

The first step to victory and walking in God's abundance is confidence in the growth process of The WORD. Jesus laid it out in Mark 4, summing it up in verses 26-29:

And he said, So is the kingdom of God, as if a man should cast seed into the ground; and should sleep, and rise night and day, and the seed should spring and grow up, he knoweth not how. For the earth bringeth forth fruit of herself; first the blade, then the ear, after that the full corn in the ear. But when the fruit is [ripe], immediately he putteth in the sickle, because the harvest is come.

Notice the confidence in the growth process displayed by the man who sowed the seed. Remember, too, we're talking about the seed being The WORD of God. It will produce if allowed to run its full course. Let's look at it like this:

1. The Seed—Find promises that cover your situation and exercise your faith. Believe you receive, and plant that WORD in your heart.
2. Rest and Praise—The sower in verse 27 did not lay awake at night worrying about whether or not the seed was growing. Don't allow the devil to talk you out of resting in faith.
3. The Blade—This is the first sign that the miracle is alive. It's doing what it's supposed to do. Stay with it.
4. The Ear—Now it's beginning to look like corn. Remember, there's more going on beneath the soil than on top: roots, strength. Stay with rest and praise.
5. The Full Ear of Corn—It really looks good! Don't pick it while it's still green. Let it develop and ripen. Don't try to make something happen, like going into debt, etc. Rest and praise.
6. It's Ripe. Harvest It!—You'll know! The dream in your heart has taken upon itself faith, and it will be born.

Once you've sown the seed of The WORD in your inner man, don't let it go. Read through Mark 4:14-20 and make note of five things that Jesus said the devil would use to try and stop the process. He has nothing new. He's the same ol' devil, and you can stop him at every turn.

This is the way the 25 percent, who won their victories and received 30, 60 and a hundredfold, got there. God is no respecter of persons. Neither is His WORD. They all had the same opportunity, because it was The WORD that brought its own harvest. The WORD works when it's put to work. Faith works. The Name of Jesus works.

There is a miracle in you right now crying to be born. All it needs is the seed of life—faith—the law of the Spirit of life in Christ Jesus.

Rise up and take your place in this mighty outpouring of the Father's glory. It's happening now. Jump in! Get together with other believers. Get into The WORD. Minister to your neighbors.

As you finish this LifeLine Kit and continue your journey of faith, put the steps I've outlined above into practice in every area of your life, and share the message of faith with other people in need. Let them know God wants them to live abundant lives, too!

Morning
Reflection

How is faith the doorway to abundance?

_____
_____
_____
_____

What is the first step to victory, every time?

_____
_____
_____
_____

According to Mark 4:14-20, what are five things Jesus said the devil would use to try to stop your sowing and harvesting process?

_____
_____
_____
_____

Today's
Connection Points

⦿ *Faith That Can Move Mountains* **CD: "We Have Overcome" (Track 10)**

Your victory has already been won! Let your faith be strengthened as you praise God for the work He's done on your behalf.

⦿ **DVD: "Your Life of Faith" (Chapter 10)**

You have been anointed to do the same works, and even greater than, Jesus did. Learn to walk in the reality and power of the Anointed One who lives in *you!*

⦿ *Faith Scriptures* **CD (Track 10)**

Colossians 2:9-10; 1 Peter 1:23; Mark 4:26-29; 1 Corinthians 13:13; Mark 4:30-32; Luke 17:1-10

Faith in Action

See yourself with your breakthrough, right now. What does it look like?

Begin acting and talking as though it has already come to pass…and soon, it will…by faith!

Notes:

_____

_____

_____

_____

_____

_____

_____

_____

_____

_____

_____

_____

_____

_____

_____

_____

_____

_____

_____

_____

_____

_____

_____

_____

_____

_____

_____

_____

_____

_____

_____

Make a Living by Faith
by Kenneth Copeland

As we wrap up our teaching in this LifeLine Kit, let's continue looking at becoming a grower of faith—because that's *so* important if you want to have an abundant life in every way possible.

The WORD says the just shall live by faith. What the world calls "making a living," or drawing a paycheck, is actually your source of seed. God wants you to use this money to sow into the kingdom of God. Second Corinthians 9:9-10 tells us that our Father ministers seed to us:

> (As it is written, He hath dispersed abroad; he hath given to the poor: his righteousness remaineth for ever. Now he that ministereth seed to the sower both minister bread for your food, and multiply your seed sown, and increase the fruits of your righteousness.)

As our Father blesses us in our jobs and as we seek first the kingdom of God and His righteousness, these things—seed, bread and the multiplying of our seed—are added to us. But faith continues to play a part. All of this is developed by the force of faith. That's what we do—*we grow faith.*

Without faith, we, just like the world, are left to live on just the seed, or from paycheck to paycheck. That has never been the will of God for His family. We're to live on the *harvest* of that seed—the seed that the Father multiplies by the power of His riches in glory.

This morning I shared from Mark 4 the order for becoming a grower of faith, according to Jesus. Again, these steps are:

1. The Seed
2. Rest (in faith)
3. The Blade (first evidence the seed is growing)
4. The Ear
5. The Full Corn in the Ear (Don't pick it green!)
6. Harvest

Let's talk more about the time of the seed. This is the most vulnerable time because there's no natural evidence the seed is growing. This is when faith is all you have to know that your breakthrough will come. But remember two keys you've learned: 1. Faith comes by hearing and hearing by The WORD of our Father, and 2. Faith works by love.

Keep your focus on your seed. Read what The WORD has to say about your situation and believe it. Commit Scripture to memory by quoting it aloud over and over and over, and by saying every time, "I choose to believe The WORD of God. I'm a believer. I have faith."

Control your mind with the verses you're standing on: "I'm a believer. I choose what to believe and what not to believe, and I believe my Father's WORD, in Jesus' Name!" Then, rest on it in your spirit.

During this time "see" yourself with it. Let your dream machine go to work. Bathe your imagination with the scriptures the Holy Spirit has given you for your breakthrough. Imagine yourself in the middle of your dream.

Somewhere along the way, the dream will begin to take faith upon itself. You'll notice yourself beginning to expect your breakthrough to come to pass. That's when the dream becomes HOPE!

"And now abide (or lives) faith, HOPE, love" (1 Corinthians 13:13). Remember, the kind of hope I'm talking about is not the same thing as a wish. A wish is the world's idea of hope. Bible hope is intense expectation that it's coming to pass, now.

Begin acting and talking as though your victory has already come to pass because in the spirit, it has. By this time, your faith is transferring what is already done in the spirit world over into the natural world where you need it.

When fear tries to rise up, remember Jairus in Luke 8 (see Chapter 2 of this Kit). DON'T LET FEAR IN! BELIEVE ONLY! Jesus promised in Mark 4:30-32 that your faith would grow up and become greater. Believe Him. It will.

Then, get out of yourself. This is so important! Jesus has a perfect plan that is glorious and superabundant, and it has your name on it. But, the only way to get into it is by faith, which works by love.

Begin helping someone else receive. Take what you've learned in this study beyond yourself. Support someone else's dream. Don't wait until you can start big. Start right where you are. Small beginnings are giant blessings when mixed with faith and love. God's in it. That's big.

Go back over Mark 4:14-32 and Luke 17:1-10. Meditate on each verse again and again. Your faith will explode into action…and *that's* living an abundant life!

Evening
Reflection

What does it mean for your income to be your "source of seed"? How does that differ from your "harvest"?

_____

_____

_____

_____

What is the growth process of your faith for abundance?

_____

_____

_____

_____

What is the evidence your seed is growing?

_____

_____

_____

_____

Notes:

_____

_____

_____

_____

_____

_____

_____

_____

_____

_____

_____

_____

_____

_____

Today's Prayer of Faith

Father, today I see my victory with the eyes of faith. My faith is the substance of what I hope for! It's the evidence of what my physical eyes cannot yet see. It's working—I know it because I have faith, and that's what it does. Praise God!

Real-Life Testimonies
to Help Build Your Faith

God Is Faithful

I just got a job after being out of work for 21 months. God has delivered me! On those CDs you sent me from the convention last year, a minister said, "Put down what you want as the ideal job. Expect God to give that to you, and don't take any less." So I did. When I got this job, I pulled out that card. Everything I wanted was in the job I got.

People scoffed at me (even my own God-fearing family!). I won't say it was easy. I was under a lot of pressure! But I had gotten some verses out of the Bible, and I read them out loud every day. I always felt better after that. I struggled to keep my mind on The LORD, and not the problem.

But what I kept hearing you say every day on TV was to do it this way and God will be faithful and deliver you. He has! Thank you so much. I love you and Gloria!

J.J.
Florida

In what three areas has your faith grown the most from your use of all the LifeLine materials in this kit?

1.

2.

3.

What are three ways you are putting your faith into action right now?

1.

2.

3.

As your faith has grown, what are three ways you can be a blessing to others this week?

1.

2.

3.

Appendix A

Scriptures and Confessions

Based on God's WORD

These can also be found on your Faith in Action Cards.

Hebrews 11:6; 2 Corinthians 5:7

Without faith it is impossible to please God, so I walk by faith in God's WORD and not by what I see, hear or feel.

Proverbs 3:5

I will trust in The LORD with my whole heart and lean not to my own understanding.

Romans 12:3

God has given to every man the measure of faith. I have faith!

Romans 10:17

My faith comes by what I hear…and today, I choose to hear The WORD of God!

Mark 11:22-23

I have faith in God. I believe, without doubting, the things I say come to pass. I speak to mountains that are in my way…and they move!

Galatians 5:6; 1 Corinthians 13:8

My faith works by love…and love *never* fails.

Hebrews 6:12

With my faith and patience working together, I inherit the promises of God!

Proverbs 28:20

I am faithful, and I abound with blessings!

Romans 8:2

The law of the Spirit of life in Christ Jesus has made me free from the law of sin and death.

Hebrews 11:1

Faith is the substance of the things I hope for, the evidence of what my physical eyes don't yet see!

Appendix B
Faith Scriptures

God wants you to have faith that is rock solid—faith that permeates every part of your life. In addition to the prayers and confessions on your Faith in Action Cards, here are more scriptures you can study and stand on as you believe God for *Faith That Can Move Mountains!*

Faith Scriptures

Habakkuk 2:4, *New Living Translation*

Look at the proud! They trust in themselves, and their lives are crooked. But the righteous will live by their faithfulness to God.

Mark 9:23

Jesus said unto him, If thou canst believe, all things are possible to him that believeth.

John 14:12

Verily, verily, I say unto you, He that believeth on me, the works that I do shall he do also; and greater works than these shall he do; because I go unto my Father.

Romans 3:27

Where is boasting then? It is excluded. By what law? of works? Nay: but by the law of faith.

Romans 4:3

For what saith the scripture? Abraham believed God, and it was counted unto him for righteousness.

Romans 4:18-21

[Abraham] against hope believed in hope, that he might become the father of many nations, according to that which was spoken, So shall thy seed be. And being not weak in faith, he considered not his own body now dead, when he was about an hundred years old, neither yet the deadness of Sarah's womb: He staggered not at the promise of God through unbelief; but was strong in faith, giving glory to God; and being fully persuaded that, what he had promised, he was able also to perform.

Romans 5:1-2

Therefore being justified by faith, we have peace with God through our LORD Jesus Christ: By whom also we have access by faith into this grace wherein we stand, and rejoice in hope of the glory of God.

2 Corinthians 4:18

While we look not at the things which are seen, but at the things which are not seen: for the things which are seen are temporal; but the things which are not seen are eternal.

Ephesians 2:8, *The Amplified Bible*

For it is by free grace (God's unmerited favor) that you are saved (delivered from judgment and made partakers of Christ's salvation) through [your] faith. And this [salvation] is not of yourselves [of your own doing, it came not through your own striving], but it is the gift of God.

Ephesians 6:16

Above all, taking the shield of faith, wherewith ye shall be able to quench all the fiery darts of the wicked.

Philippians 4:13

I can do all things through Christ which strengtheneth me.

Hebrews 10:23

Let us hold fast the profession of our faith without wavering; (for he is faithful that promised).

Hebrews 10:39, *The Amplified Bible*

But our way is not that of those who draw back to eternal misery (perdition) and are utterly destroyed, but we are of those who believe [who cleave to and trust in and rely on God through Jesus Christ, the Messiah] and by faith preserve the soul.

Hebrews 11:3

Through faith we understand that the worlds were framed by The WORD of God, so that things which are seen were not made of things which do appear.

James 1:2-4

My brethren, count it all joy when ye fall into divers temptations; knowing this, that the trying of your faith worketh patience. But let patience have her perfect work, that ye may be perfect and entire, wanting nothing.

James 2:14

What doth it profit, my brethren, though a man say he hath faith, and have not works? can faith save him?

James 2:17

Even so faith, if it hath not works, is dead, being alone.

James 2:26

For as the body without the spirit is dead, so faith without works is dead also.

Titus 2:2

That the aged men be sober, grave, temperate, sound in faith, in charity, in patience.

Love Scriptures

Matthew 22:37

Jesus said unto him, Thou shalt love The LORD thy God with all thy heart, and with all thy soul, and with all thy mind.

John 14:21

He that hath my commandments, and keepeth them, he it is that loveth me: and he that loveth me shall be loved of my Father, and I will love him, and will manifest myself to him.

John 17:26

And I have declared unto them thy name, and will declare it: that the love wherewith thou hast loved me may be in them, and I in them.

1 Corinthians 13:1-8, *The Amplified Bible*

If I [can] speak in the tongues of men and [even] of angels, but have not love (that reasoning, intentional, spiritual devotion such as is inspired by God's love for and in us), I am only a noisy gong or a clanging cymbal. And if I have prophetic powers (the gift of interpreting the divine will and purpose), and understand all the secret truths and mysteries and possess all knowledge, and if I have [sufficient] faith so that I can remove mountains, but have not love (God's love in me) I am nothing (a useless nobody). Even if I dole out all that I have [to the poor in providing] food, and if I surrender my body to be burned or in order that I may glory, but have not love (God's love in me), I gain nothing. Love endures long and is patient and kind; love never is envious nor boils over with jealousy, is not boastful or vainglorious, does not display itself haughtily. It is not conceited (arrogant and inflated with pride); it is not rude (unmannerly) and does not act unbecomingly. Love (God's love in us) does not insist on its own rights or its own way, for it is not self-seeking; it is not touchy or fretful or resentful; it takes no account of the evil done to it [it pays no attention to a suffered wrong]. It does not rejoice at injustice and unrighteousness, but rejoices when right and truth prevail. Love bears up under anything and everything that comes, is ever ready to believe the best of every person, its hopes are fadeless under all circumstances, and it endures everything [without weakening]. Love never fails [never fades out or becomes obsolete or comes to an end]....

1 Corinthians 13:13

And now abideth faith, hope, charity, these three; but the greatest of these is charity.

Colossians 2:2-3

That their hearts might be comforted, being knit together in love, and unto all riches of the full assurance of understanding, to the acknowledgement of the mystery of God, and of the Father, and of Christ; in whom are hid all the treasures of wisdom and knowledge.

James 3:16

For where envying and strife is, there is confusion and every evil work.

1 John 4:15-16

Whosoever shall confess that Jesus is the Son of God, God dwelleth in him, and he in God. And we have known and believed the love that God hath to us. God is love; and he that dwelleth in love dwelleth in God, and God in him.

1 John 5:1-5

Whosoever believeth that Jesus is the Christ is born of God: and every one that loveth him that begat loveth him also that is begotten of him. By this we know that we love the children of God, when we love God, and keep his commandments. For this is the love of God, that we keep his commandments: and his commandments are not grievous. For whatsoever is born of God overcometh the world: and this is the victory that overcometh the world, even our faith. Who is he that overcometh the world, but he that believeth that Jesus is the Son of God?

Promises From God's WORD

Joshua 1:7-8, *The Amplified Bible*

Only you be strong and very courageous, that you may do according to all the law which Moses My servant commanded you. Turn not from it to the right hand or to the left, that you may prosper wherever you go. This Book of the Law shall not depart out of your mouth, but you shall meditate on it day and night, that you may observe and do according to all that is written in it. For then you shall make your way prosperous, and then you shall deal wisely and have good success.

Psalm 91

He that dwelleth in the secret place of the most High shall abide under the shadow of the Almighty. I will say of The LORD, He is my refuge and my fortress: my God; in him will I trust. Surely he shall deliver thee from the snare of the fowler, and from the noisome pestilence. He shall cover thee with his feathers, and under his wings shalt thou trust: his truth shall be thy shield and buckler. Thou shalt not be afraid for the terror by night; nor for the arrow that flieth by day; nor for the pestilence that walketh in darkness; nor for the destruction that wasteth at noonday. A thousand shall fall at thy side, and ten thousand at thy right hand; but it shall not come nigh thee. Only with thine eyes shalt thou behold and see the reward of the wicked. Because thou hast made The LORD, which is my refuge, even the most High, thy habitation; there shall no evil befall thee, neither shall any plague come nigh thy dwelling. For he shall give his angels charge over thee, to keep thee in all thy ways. They shall bear thee up in their hands, lest thou dash thy foot against a stone. Thou shalt tread upon the lion and adder: the young lion and the dragon shalt thou trample under feet. Because he hath set his love upon me, therefore will I deliver him: I will set him on high, because he hath known my name. He shall call upon me, and I will answer him: I will be with him in trouble; I will deliver him, and honour him. With long life will I satisfy him, and show him my salvation.

Proverbs 4:20-23

My son, attend to my words; incline thine ear unto my sayings. Let them not depart from thine eyes; keep them in the midst of thine heart. For they are life unto those that find them, and health to all their flesh. Keep thy heart with all diligence; for out of it are the issues of life.

Proverbs 6:20-22

My son, keep thy father's commandment, and forsake not the law of thy mother: Bind them continually upon thine heart, and tie them about thy neck. When thou goest, it shall lead thee; when thou sleepest, it shall keep thee; and when thou awakest, it shall talk with thee.

Isaiah 53:4-5

Surely he hath borne our griefs, and carried our sorrows: yet we did esteem him stricken, smitten of God, and afflicted. But he was wounded for our transgressions, he was bruised for our iniquities: the chastisement of our peace was upon him; and with his stripes we are healed.

Isaiah 55:10-11, *The Amplified Bible*

For as the rain and snow come down from the heavens, and return not there again, but water the earth and make it bring forth and sprout, that it may give seed to the sower and bread to the eater, so shall My WORD be that goes forth out of My mouth: it shall not return to Me void [without producing any effect, useless], but it shall accomplish that which I please and purpose, and it shall prosper in the thing for which I sent it.

Mark 4:14-32

The sower soweth The WORD. And these are they by the way side, where The WORD is sown; but when they have heard, Satan cometh immediately, and taketh away The WORD that was sown in their hearts. And these are they likewise which are sown on stony ground; who, when they have heard The WORD, immediately receive it with gladness; and have no root in themselves, and so endure but for a time: afterward, when affliction or persecution ariseth for The WORD's sake, immediately they are offended. And these are they which are sown among thorns; such as hear The WORD, and the cares of this world, and the deceitfulness of riches, and the lusts of other things entering in, choke The WORD, and it becometh unfruitful. And these are they which are sown on good ground; such as hear The WORD, and receive it, and bring forth fruit, some thirtyfold, some sixty, and some an hundred. And he said unto them, Is a candle brought to be put under a bushel, or under a bed? and not to be set on a candlestick? For there is nothing hid, which shall not be manifested; neither was any thing kept secret, but that it should come abroad. If any man have ears to hear, let him hear. And he said unto them, Take heed what ye hear: with what measure ye mete, it shall be measured to you: and unto you that hear shall more be given. For he that hath, to him shall be given: and he that hath not, from him shall be taken even that which he hath. And he said, So is the kingdom of God, as if a man should cast seed into the ground; and should sleep, and rise night and day, and the seed should spring and grow up, he knoweth not how. For the earth bringeth forth fruit of herself; first the blade, then the ear, after that the full corn in the ear. But when the fruit is brought forth, immediately he putteth in the sickle, because the harvest is come. And he said, Whereunto shall we liken the kingdom of God? or with what comparison shall we compare it? It is like a grain of mustard seed, which, when it is sown in the earth, is less than all the seeds that be in the earth: But when it is sown, it groweth up, and becometh greater than all herbs, and shooteth out great branches; so that the fowls of the air may lodge under the shadow of it.

John 6:63

It is the spirit that quickeneth; the flesh profiteth nothing: the words that I speak unto you, they are spirit, and they are life.

1 Corinthians 1:9

God is faithful, by whom ye were called unto the fellowship of his Son Jesus Christ our LORD.

Hebrews 4:12, *The Amplified Bible*

For The WORD that God speaks is alive and full of power [making it active, operative, energizing, and effective]; it is sharper than any two-edged sword, penetrating to the dividing line of the breath of life (soul) and [the immortal] spirit, and of joints and marrow [of the deepest parts of our nature], exposing and sifting and analyzing and judging the very thoughts and purposes of the heart.

Hebrews 13:5, *The Amplified Bible*

He [God] Himself has said, I will not in any way fail you nor give you up nor leave you without support. [I will] not, [I will] not, [I will] not in any degree leave you helpless nor forsake nor let [you] down (relax My hold on you)! [Assuredly not!]

1 Peter 1:23

Being born again, not of corruptible seed, but of incorruptible, by The WORD of God, which liveth and abideth for ever.

Redemption Scriptures

Deuteronomy 30:19-20

I call heaven and earth to record this day against you, that I have set before you life and death, blessing and cursing: therefore choose life, that both thou and thy seed may live: that thou mayest love The LORD thy God, and that thou mayest obey his voice, and that thou mayest cleave unto him: for he is thy life, and the length of thy days: that thou mayest dwell in the land which The LORD sware unto thy fathers, to Abraham, to Isaac, and to Jacob, to give them.

Isaiah 53:4-5

Surely he [Jesus] hath borne our griefs, and carried our sorrows: yet we did esteem him stricken, smitten of God, and afflicted. But he was wounded for our transgressions, he was bruised for our iniquities: the chastisement of our peace was upon him; and with his stripes we are healed.

Romans 8:1-2

There is therefore now no condemnation to them which are in Christ Jesus, who walk not after the flesh, but after the Spirit. For the law of the Spirit of life in Christ Jesus hath made me free from the law of sin and death.

Galatians 3:13-14

Christ hath redeemed us from the curse of the law, being made a curse for us: for it is written, Cursed is every one that hangeth on a tree: that the blessing of Abraham might come on the Gentiles through Jesus Christ; that we might receive the promise of the Spirit through faith.

Philippians 4:19

But my God shall supply all your need according to his riches in glory by Christ Jesus.

1 Peter 2:24

Who his own self bare our sins in his own body on the tree, that we, being dead to sins, should live unto righteousness: by whose stripes ye were healed.

Confession Scriptures

Joshua 1:8

This book of the law shall not depart out of thy mouth; but thou shalt meditate therein day and night, that thou mayest observe to do according to all that is written therein: for then thou shalt make thy way prosperous, and then thou shalt have good success.

Matthew 12:33-35, *New International Version*

Make a tree good and its fruit will be good, or make a tree bad and its fruit will be bad, for a tree is recognized by its fruit. You brood of vipers, how can you who are evil say anything good? For the mouth speaks what the heart is full of. A good man brings good things out of the good stored up in him, and an evil man brings evil things out of the evil stored up in him.

Mark 11:22-25

And Jesus answering saith unto them, Have faith in God. For verily I say unto you, That whosoever shall say unto this mountain, Be thou removed, and be thou cast into the sea; and shall not doubt in his heart, but shall believe that those things which he saith shall come to pass; he shall have whatsoever he saith. Therefore I say unto you, What things soever ye desire, when ye pray, believe that ye receive them, and ye shall have them. And when ye stand praying, forgive, if ye have aught against any: that your Father also which is in heaven may forgive you your trespasses.

James 3:6-8

And the tongue is a fire, a world of iniquity: so is the tongue among our members, that it defileth the whole body, and setteth on fire the course of nature; and it is set on fire of hell. For every kind of beasts, and of birds, and of serpents, and of things in the sea, is tamed, and hath been tamed of mankind: But the tongue can no man tame; it is an unruly evil, full of deadly poison.

Appendix C
Prayers and
Confessions of Faith

Personal Prayer of Faith

Father, in the Name of Jesus, I choose life, today! I choose to walk in faith and not fear. Because You, LORD, are on my side, *I will not fear* what anyone can do to me. LORD, open my eyes to any hidden areas of fear in my life. I will fill my heart and mouth with Your WORD so I can walk in faith to receive all You have for me.

Your WORD says faith comes by hearing The WORD of God. I will build up my faith today by reading, meditating and acting on Your WORD. Thank You, Father, for the hedge of protection that surrounds me and my loved ones according to Psalm 91. Thank You that through the righteousness of Jesus I can confidently trust in Your peace and safety for my life and home knowing that Your angels are always on guard. I believe I receive Your peace and protection for me and my loved ones, today! In Jesus' Name. Amen.

References: Deuteronomy 30:19; 2 Corinthians 5:7; Psalm 118:6; Romans 10:17; Job 1:10; Isaiah 32:17-18 *(The Amplified Bible)*; Psalms 34:7, 91:11

Prayer of Faith for Others

Heavenly Father, I cease not to pray for _____, that You grant him/her a spirit of wisdom and revelation and insight into mysteries and secrets—in the deep and intimate knowledge of You, having the eyes of his/her heart flooded with light so that he/she can know and understand the hope to which You have called him/her, and to know how rich Your glorious inheritance is in the saints and what is the exceeding greatness of Your power toward us who believe.

I pray that _____ walks, lives and conducts himself/herself in a manner worthy of You, fully pleasing to You and desiring to please You in all things, bearing fruit in every good work and steadily growing and increasing in the knowledge of You. I pray that he/she may be invigorated and strengthened with all power by Your Spirit to exercise every kind of endurance and patience, perseverance and forbearance with joy.

I believe the good work You began in _____ will continue, right up to the time of Jesus' return, perfecting it and bringing it to its full completion in him/her, in Jesus' Name. Amen.

References: Ephesians 1:17-19; Colossians 1:10-11; Philippians 1:6

Confession to Receive

I'm not moved by what I see, hear, feel or experience. I'm only moved by what I believe. I believe The WORD of God. I have the God-kind of faith. God's WORD is in my heart and in my mouth. I have spoken my faith, and I believe I receive _____. I have it now. I see it with the eye of my faith, according to The WORD of God, and I rejoice that it is mine by faith!

Thank You, LORD, that I have a great High Priest in heaven, Jesus, the Christ, the Son of the living God, and He said I can have whatsoever I say (Mark 11:23-24). So, out of the abundance of my heart, I speak The WORD of God over my situation, knowing that His WORD *never* fails. I believe I receive it now, when I pray. It *shall* come to pass!

References: Romans 10:8; Mark 11:23-24; James 2:17; Hebrews 4:14-16; Matthew 12:34-35

"Moving Mountains" Confession

I do as Jesus did, and I speak to the mountain of _____ in my life. I command _____ to be removed from my (life, body, relationship, job) and to be cast into the sea, and away from me and my loved ones! I believe I receive it removed, by faith, in the Name of Jesus.

I have no doubt in my mind that I am free from _____. No weapons of fear, doubt or unbelief formed against me shall prosper. I call those things that are not as though they were and hope for what I do not have, waiting patiently in faith, believing with great expectation, for it to come to pass in my life.

References: Mark 11:23-25; Isaiah 54:17; Romans 4:17, 8:25

"My Faith Works!" Confession

I hear, study, believe, receive and confess God's WORD, and my faith continues to grow. I abide in God, and His WORD abides in me. So, I ask for what I need according to His WORD, and I believe I receive it by faith. Jesus is LORD over my situation, and I do not fear or worry about what I'm going through because I released my faith, and God's will is being done in my life right now.

Jesus is the author and finisher of my faith, so I look unto Him by believing and acting on His WORD! I believe my faith works because I believe God's WORD is true; it comes to pass in my life because He is the rewarder of those who seek Him. I hear The WORD, I receive it and I act on it by faith. I do not doubt. I believe in my heart, according to Mark 11:23-24 that I have what I spoke by faith.

References: Romans 10:17; John 15:7; Mark 11:23-24; Hebrews 12:2, 11:6; James 2:17

Additional Materials to Help You Stir Up Faith That Can Move Mountains

Books

- From Faith to Faith Devotional
- The Unbeatable Spirit of Faith
- Faith and Confession
- Dream Big, Talk Big, and Turn Your Faith Loose
- Faith and Patience: The Power Twins

Audio Resources

- Faith: How It Works
- Faith School
- How to Put Your Faith to Work
- Faith Series
- Consistency: The Powerhouse of Faith
- The Spirit of Faith
- Hope: The Blueprint of Faith
- Faith and Patience
- Faith in God's Love
- Faith Opens Prison Doors
- Developing Fully Persuaded Faith
- Words of Prayer, Words of Faith
- Faith Like a Rock

Video Resources

- Prayer Series 7: The Prayer of Faith

Prayer for Salvation and Baptism in the Holy Spirit

Heavenly Father, I come to You in the Name of Jesus. Your Word says, "Whosoever shall call on the name of the Lord shall be saved" (Acts 2:21). I am calling on You. I pray and ask Jesus to come into my heart and be Lord over my life according to Romans 10:9-10: "If thou shalt confess with thy mouth the Lord Jesus, and shalt believe in thine heart that God hath raised him from the dead, thou shalt be saved. For with the heart man believeth unto righteousness; and with the mouth confession is made unto salvation." I do that now. I confess that Jesus is Lord, and I believe in my heart that God raised Him from the dead.

I am now reborn! I am a Christian—a child of Almighty God! I am saved! You also said in Your Word, "If ye then, being evil, know how to give good gifts unto your children: HOW MUCH MORE shall your heavenly Father give the Holy Spirit to them that ask him?" (Luke 11:13). I'm also asking You to fill me with the Holy Spirit. Holy Spirit, rise up within me as I praise God. I fully expect to speak with other tongues as You give me the utterance (Acts 2:4). In Jesus' Name. Amen!

Begin to praise God for filling you with the Holy Spirit. Speak those words and syllables you receive—not in your own language, but the language given to you by the Holy Spirit. You have to use your own voice. God will not force you to speak. Don't be concerned with how it sounds. It is a heavenly language!

Continue with the blessing God has given you and pray in the spirit every day.

You are a born-again, Spirit-filled believer. You'll never be the same!

Find a good church that boldly preaches God's Word and obeys it. Become part of a church family who will love and care for you as you love and care for them.

We need to be connected to each other. It increases our strength in God. It's God's plan for us.

Make it a habit to watch the *Believer's Voice of Victory* television broadcast and become a doer of the Word, who is blessed in his doing (James 1:22-25).

About the Authors

Kenneth and Gloria Copeland are the best-selling authors of more than 60 books. They have also co-authored numerous books including *Family Promises,* the *LifeLine* series and *From Faith to Faith—A Daily Guide to Victory.* As founders of Kenneth Copeland Ministries in Fort Worth, Texas, Kenneth and Gloria have been circling the globe with the uncompromised Word of God since 1967, preaching and teaching a lifestyle of victory for every Christian.

Their daily and Sunday *Believer's Voice of Victory* television broadcasts now air on more than 500 stations around the world, and the *Believer's Voice of Victory* magazine is distributed to nearly 600,000 believers worldwide. Kenneth Copeland Ministries' international prison ministry reaches more than 20,000 new inmates every year and receives more than 20,000 pieces of correspondence each month. Their teaching materials can also be found on the World Wide Web. With offices and staff in the United States, Canada, England, Australia, South Africa, Ukraine and Singapore, Kenneth and Gloria's teaching materials—books, magazines, audios and videos—have been translated into at least 26 languages to reach the world with the love of God.

We're Here for You!®

Your growth in God's WORD and victory in Jesus are at the very center of our hearts. In every way God has equipped us, we will help you deal with the issues facing you, so you can be the **victorious overcomer** He has planned for you to be.

The mission of Kenneth Copeland Ministries is about all of us growing and going together. Our prayer is that you will take full advantage of all The LORD has given us to share with you.

Wherever you are in the world, you can watch the *Believer's Voice of Victory* broadcast on television (check your local listings), the Internet at kcm.org or on our digital Roku channel.

Our website, **kcm.org,** gives you access to every resource we've developed for your victory. And, you can find contact information for our international offices in Africa, Asia, Australia, Canada, Europe, Ukraine and our headquarters in the United States.

Each office is staffed with devoted men and women, ready to serve and pray with you. You can contact the worldwide office nearest you for assistance, and you can call us for prayer at our U.S. number, +1-817-852-6000, 24 hours every day!

We encourage you to connect with us often and let us be part of your everyday walk of faith!

Jesus Is LORD!

Kenneth & Gloria Copeland

Kenneth and Gloria Copeland